Brighton & Hove

Brighton & Hove

Matthew Andrews   Max Crisfield

F

FRANCES LINCOLN LIMITED

PUBLISHERS

www.franceslincoln.com

For Jo & Dona

Acknowledgments

We would like to thank the following people and organisations for their kind assistance and for allowing access to their buildings:

Archer's Butchers; Audrey's Chocolates; Austin Rees, former Municipal Technical College, Richmond Terrace; Brighton College; British Engineerium; Churchill Square; Bluestorm Ltd, Embassy Court; Brighton Dome; Brighton Hippodrome; De Vere Grand Hotel; Gwydyr Salon; Komedia; Mike Laslett; The Old Ship Hotel; Royal Pavilion, Libraries and Museums, Brighton & Hove Council; St Andrew's Church; St Bartholomew's Church; Church of St John the Baptist; St Michael & All Angels Church; St Nicholas Church; First Base Day Centre, St Stephen's Hall; Southern Trains, Brighton Railway Station; Southern Water, Brighton Sewers; Regency Town House; Theatre Royal Brighton; and S.R. Peek, whose pictures were an early inspiration.

Authors' Note

Brighton and Hove councils were merged to form a single unitary authority in 1997 and the combined city of Brighton & Hove was born on the eve of the new millennium. However, for brevity's sake, the city is referred to as Brighton throughout this book, unless express reference is made to the historic resort town of Hove itself.

Frances Lincoln Ltd
4 Torriano Mews
Torriano Avenue
London NW5 2RZ
www.franceslincoln.com

Brighton & Hove
Copyright © Frances Lincoln Ltd 2006
Photographs copyright © Matthew Andrews 2006
Text copyright © Max Crisfield 2006

Designed by Ian Hunt

British Library Cataloguing in Publication Data
A catalogue record for this book is available from the British Library.

ISBN 13: 978-0-7112-2646-3

Printed and bound in Singapore

9 8 7 6 5 4 3 2

contents

introduction   6

history   8

seafront   26

kemp town   44

montpelier, clifton hill and st nicholas church   58

the cultural quarter, royal pavilion and north laine   72

the lanes/old quarter   86

hove   100

hanover & queen's park   114

bibliography   127

index   128

introduction

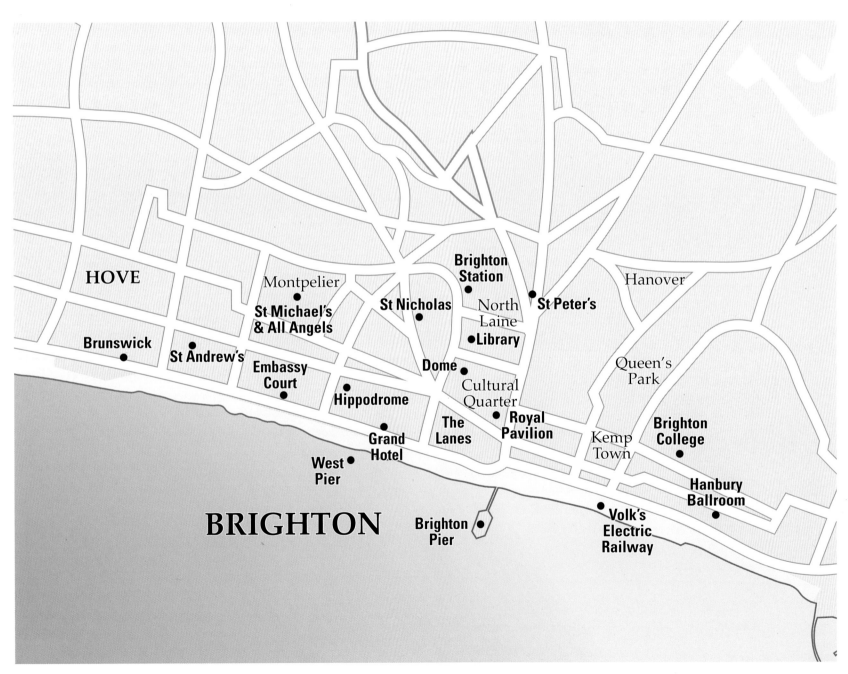

HOVE

Montpelier

Brighton
Station

Hanover

St Nicholas

North
Laine

St Peter's

St Michael's
& All Angels

Library

Brunswick

St Andrew's

Embassy
Court

Dome

Queen's
Park

Cultural
Quarter

Hippodrome

Royal
Pavilion

Brighton
College

The
Lanes

Kemp
Town

Grand
Hotel

West
Pier

BRIGHTON

Brighton
Pier

Volk's
Electric
Railway

Hanbury
Ballroom

Every city has its instant identifiers: Canterbury's Cathedral, Oxford's spires, Edinburgh's Castle. Brighton is a city replete with grand architectural gestures and iconic images, dreamed up by princes and celebrated by pleasure-seekers for almost three centuries. For many visitors, the onion-domed opulence of the Royal Pavilion, the seafront esplanade, the sweep of the Regency terraces and the sideshow kitsch of the Victorian piers add up to quintessential Brighton.

But this is just one part of the story. Wander away from the city centre in any direction for a short distance and the true heart of Brighton begins to be revealed. From the stately grandeur of Clifton Hill to Hove's nineteenth-century 'new town', Brunswick; from Kemp Town's colourful eccentricities to Hanover's churches and ale-houses, Brighton is a collection of distinct environs. These are defined as much by their characters and customs as the architecture and history that gives them their unique flavour.

While revisiting Brighton's classic landmarks, this book also heads off the beaten track, embarking on a photographic journey across the city's lesser known quarters. In so doing it seeks out the stories, discovering along the way how this grand dame of decadence grew from sleepy fishing village to bustling metropolis in a classic coming-of-age tale.

It is, of course, impossible to tell the whole story, to turn every stone and capture every nuance. Brighton has, tucked away across its length and breadth, enough images and stories to fill this volume twice over. Such is the challenge where every street corner, alleyway or avenue affords another visual encounter with the city's narrative. However, the seven districts presented together here make up the heart and soul of the city, each providing a taste of its architectural, cultural and historical evolution.

Photography, at its most effective, provides a fresh pair of eyes. It frames the familiar in an entirely new way, so as to make us stand back and look again. At the same time it brings the unfamiliar to our attention, encouraging us to seek out its secrets. This book offers a new perspective from which to re-imagine the city's familiar landscapes. For those to whom the city is as yet undiscovered, we hope that the book will also provide a visual roadmap with which to explore and unearth its numerous treasures.

ABOVE LEFT **Deckchairs, Brighton Beach**

ABOVE RIGHT **Bank holiday weekend, Brighton beach**

history

'In Lydia's imagination a visit to Brighton comprised every possibility of earthly happiness.'

Jane Austen, *Pride and Prejudice*

Brighton is a city where nothing is quite as it appears. A stone's throw from the Continent, one minute it seems like an undiscovered corner of Europe, the next it reminds you of its quintessential Englishness. It is a city of improbable makeovers and deft sleight of hand: farmhouses transformed into palaces, stable blocks into concert halls, churches into art galleries. It is a city of bus-driving poets and saxophone-playing maître d's; a place where waiters await that elusive three-book publishing deal, and where the underground comes up to the surface for air.

Unlike most seaside resorts, it is a year-round city: buoyed up by two universities and a thriving arts and culture scene. It boasts the biggest arts festival in England, and its most celebrated gay scene. It's got 5 miles of coastline, 23 parks, 5 casinos, 20 bowling greens, 3,450 listed buildings, 12 theatres, 26 lifeguards, 30 nightclubs, 20 art galleries, and more restaurants per head of population than anywhere else in the United Kingdom outside of London.

It has taken a star turn in a raft of literary classics – Jane Austen's *Pride and Prejudice*, William Thackeray's *Vanity Fair*, Charles Dickens' *Dombey and Son*, Evelyn Waugh's *Handful of Dust* and even a walk-on part in T.S. Eliot's *The Wasteland* – and has inspired equally iconic cinematic moments from *Oh! What a Lovely War* to *Quadrophenia*.

And all of this is played out against a backdrop of bow-fronted Regency terraces, grand squares, Rococo palaces, Gothic churches, Victorian synagogues and a rash of twenty-first-century luxury loft apartments.

RIGHT **Bowls, Preston Park**

BELOW LEFT Opened in 1910, the Grade II-listed Duke of York's cinema is one of the oldest purpose-built picture houses in the country.

BELOW RIGHT Rookery Rock Garden, Preston Park, constructed from 1,350 tons of Cheddar stone, is the largest municipal rock garden in Britain.

RIGHT An Edwardian shopfront in the Port Hall area.

Of course, Brighton didn't just dream itself into its current confection in a historic vacuum. But it did undergo a miraculous transformation, pulling off one of the most audacious conjuring tricks in British history: from fishing village to 'Piccadilly by the sea' in the blink of an eye. For the story of Brighton, like all good stories, is a tale of reinvention. It is a rambunctious, episodic romp, punctuated with eccentric patrons, opportunists, visionaries and fortune-seekers all washed down with bucket-loads of serendipity. It's a rags to riches rollercoaster ride: *Great Expectations*, *Vanity Fair* and *Cinderella* rolled into one.

Brighton's history begins with a Neolithic encampment on Whitehawk Hill. The Romans also made their presence known. But it was the Anglo-Saxons who founded the first true settlement, the small fishing village of 'Brightelmstune', formed where the South Downs meet the shoreline of the English Channel on a plateau above the west bank of Brighton's 'lost river', the Wellesbourne. The origins of the name itself are ambiguous and have invited much speculation. The most likely derivation is from either Brighthelm's Tun or Beorthelm's Town – a village or farmstead belonging to a Saxon chieftain of that name.

By the time of the Norman Conquest, Brighton was conferred to the barony of Lewes and was a growing community, tithed to the annual tune of 4,000 herrings. Over the next few centuries medieval Brighton or 'Brightelmstone', grew into one of the largest fishing villages in Sussex, as it began to

spread out from the weather-beaten foreshore on to the cliff-top above. Despite constant erosion, taxes, French invasion, crop failures and bitter wrangling between fishermen and landsmen, the town prospered and by 1640 had become a significant southern fishery.

Brighton's first flirtation with celebrity was fleeting, but not insignificant. Charles II, fleeing the country after the Battle of Worcester, found himself at the mercy of Brighton's fishing community. Lodging the night at the George Inn on West Street, he made his escape from Shoreham aboard the brig *Surprise* in the company of Captain Nicolas Tettersell in the early hours of 15 October 1651. A recurring figure in Brighton history, Tettersell later sailed the *Surprise* to London and was granted a pension by Charles and a commission in the Navy. He subsequently became Constable of Brighton and an ardent persecutor of nonconformists.

This brief brush with royal favour did not precipitate the town's meteoric rise to fame and fortune, however. This honour was to lie in the hands of another monarch whose reasons

for visiting were less expedient, and whose residency brought about such a monumental shift in the town's circumstance. This, however, is jumping the gun. Following the Restoration of Charles II in 1660, Brighton fell into a seemingly irreversible decline, a profound economic slump brought about by competition from inland towns, poor communications, scarcity of raw materials, and exacerbated by a series of early eighteenth-century storms that decimated the foreshore.

On visiting the town during his *Tour Through the Whole of Great Britain*, which appeared in published form in 1724–6, Daniel Defoe was left in no doubt as to its abject circumstance: 'Brightelmstone being an old built and poor, tho' prosperous town, was miserably torn to pieces, and made the very picture of desolation, that it looked as if an enemy had sacked it.'

When Dr Richard Russell – Brighton's first catalytic impulse towards a more sanguine disposition – first made his mark on the town, it had reached its nadir. The population was depleted to 2,000, unemployment was rife, and the town was reduced to living on its own meagre resources, augmented

ABOVE The Jewish Cemetery, Meadowview, Bevendean Road

RIGHT Brighton's Extra-Mural Cemetery sits in a wide, secluded fold between Lewes Road and Bear Road. It was laid out by Amon Henry Wilds from 1851 and provides the final resting place for many of Brighton's most eminent Victorians.

13

by smuggling from the Continent. Appropriately, Brighton's first seismic shift in fortune came about not through trade or industry, but as a consequence of fashion. By the 1740s the nation was in the grip of a new panacea, a seawater cure-all expounded by eminent physicians such as Dr Russell. So popular was his treatment for a panoply of diseases, a treatment that included drinking as well as bathing in seawater, that soon Brighton was overrun with ailing converts in search of seaside convalescence.

As word spread of 'Dr Brighton's' restorative powers, the fashionable London set began to emigrate southwards. So began an exercise in gentrification on an unprecedented scale, transforming the town beyond all recognition. As the Napoleonic Wars raged across Europe, and military camps sprang up along the coast, Brighton became a grand stage set for the perambulations of generals, dukes and duchesses. It offered a social whirl of assemblies, dances, recitals and concerts: a seafront playground in which to idle away winter months in concerted loafing, gossip and social climbing.

Brighton flourished, and if there was one single event that was to define its coming of age, it was the arrival on 7 September 1783 of King George III's eldest son, George, Prince of Wales, then aged twenty-one. For the Prince, Brighton offered a refuge from the stuffy formality of the Court of St James and a release valve for frustrations brought on by familial discord. Rebellious in spirit, eccentric, charming and good looking, he was embraced by Brighton Society and found its relative freedoms a welcome tonic. However, he soon fell in with a coterie of raffish boors and idle aristocratic pranksters, tutored in the ways of dissolute living by his uncle the Duke of Cumberland, much to the chagrin of his father.

If his taste for high living and nefarious company was frowned upon by the King, then his relentless pursuit of the twice-widowed beauty Maria Fitzherbert can only have added fuel to the fire. After an eccentric cat and mouse courtship, the couple were married behind closed doors on 15 December 1785 at Mrs Fitzherbert's home in London. The secret wedding was illegal, as the Royal Marriage Act of 1772 invalidated any marriage by a member of the royal family under the age of twenty-five contracted without the consent of the King. This consent, of course, would never have been given, for not only was Mrs Fitzherbert a commoner, she was also a Roman Catholic, and an act passed eighty years earlier had decreed that no Prince married to a 'Papist' should succeed to the throne.

Though the couple never openly shared a house, and the marriage was never made official, they established themselves in Brighton at the centre of the most flamboyant season in the social calendar. Brighton had 'arrived', and could lay credible

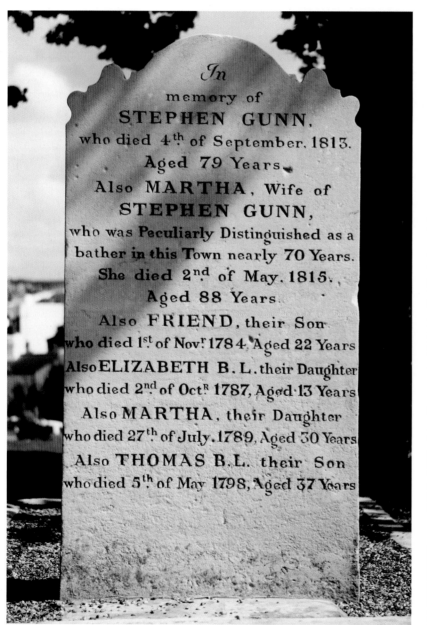

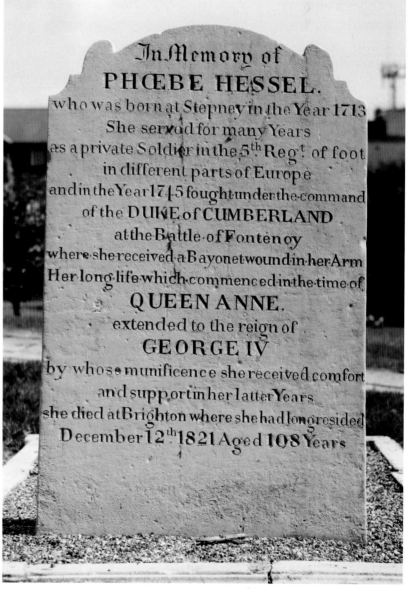

claim to being the social and fashion capital of England. Through his cook, Louis Weltje, the Prince leased a modest farmhouse on the Steine from Thomas Read Kemp in 1786. However, he soon began to make the first of a series of renovations and expansions that would transform the classically inspired Marine Pavilion into today's oriental palace.

George III showed signs of madness as early as 1788 but it was not until 1811, when the condition had become irreversible, that his son was named Regent. This tragedy for the King marked the dawning of Brighton's golden age, with a *Who's Who* of English and European aristocracy swelling the town to capacity. Its humble origins were all but forgotten, unless of course you happened to be of humble descent yourself, in which case poverty, disease, prostitution, rampant crime and cramped living conditions were part and parcel of life in the shadows of Brighton's grand façades.

Society flocked in their droves: by 1822, thirty-nine stagecoaches were making the daily journey to Brighton from London. The town responded with a dizzying display of elegant Regency architecture: cream and white crescents and bowfronted balconied terraces designed by Brighton's foremost architectural partnership, Amon Henry Wilds and Charles Augustin Busby. Strictly speaking, much of what we commonly term Regency – the elegant façades of Kemp Town and Brunswick, Montpelier and Adelaide – were in fact constructed in the 1820s and beyond, after the Regent had ascended the throne as George IV. However, the term can be loosely applied to cover a stylistic sensibility that informed the Brighton aesthetic from 1811 right through to the 1830s and '40s.

In the wake of such unprecedented wealth came the inevitable cavalcade of chancers determined to catch a piece of the action. Opportunists and conspirators mingled with minor royalty and the cream of Regency Society in an improbable cross-section. The dandy, Beau Brummel, the rakish poet,

Lord Byron, the composers Rossini and Paganini, the artists J.M.W. Turner and John Constable, all made their mark on Brighton and helped to secure its reputation as the jewel in the social crown.

George IV's coronation in 1821 marked the beginning of the end of his love affair with Brighton. Long since estranged from his beloved Mrs Fitzherbert, he had married Princess Caroline of Brunswick as an exercise in familial appeasement and debt recovery in 1795. This marriage proved a disaster, and George sought solace in the arms of a series of matronly aristocratic ladies. Grossly overweight and plagued with gout, he gradually found the pressing crowds and lack of privacy in Brighton an unwelcome intrusion – he was even afraid that he might be assassinated. Retreating with distinctly less ceremony than he had arrived, he ended his days in quiet seclusion with his last mistress, Lady Conyngham, at Windsor Castle.

The end of one era – an age defined by the relentless pursuit of pleasure – ushered in, at least on the surface, a more austere epoch in which priests took the place of princes and industrialisation paved the way for Brighton's next great act of reinvention. However, as Anthony Dale has suggested in *Fashionable Brighton & Hove*, 'the Regency reputation for rakishness died hard, and enough of its flavour persisted right through the whole of the nineteenth century to redeem Brighton from the least attractive aspects of the Victorian age.'

Key to Brighton's nineteenth-century religious revival were the 'high church' philanthropist reformers, the Rev. Henry Wagner, Vicar of Brighton from 1824 to 1870, and his son, Father Arthur Wagner, perpetual curate of the Church of St Paul. Arthur, in particular, was a central figure in the Anglo-Catholic controversy of the day, an advocate of the Oxford Movement, whose ritualist practices and 'popish' sympathies were such an affront to Brighton's 'low church' tradition of dissent and nonconformity. Opposed to the ubiquitous practice of

LEFT All 1,500 of the seats in St Bartholomew's Church were free from pew rents, hence the nickname 'Wagner's Folly'.

OPPOSITE St Bartholomew's Church. Rumoured, almost certainly apocryphally, to be constructed by local architect Edmund Scott to the dimensions of Noah's Ark, St Bartholomew's is, however, the tallest parish church in the country – its nave higher than that of Westminster Abbey. An exercise in maximum glory to God at minimal outlay, this leviathan of a church cost a mere £18,000 to build. Yet, on completion in 1874, it dwarfed everything around it for miles. So vast was it, in fact, that it caused its own microclimate, creating such a downdraft that the chimneys of the adjacent houses were perpetually choked with smoke.

pew rental to wealthy worshippers, both men fought tirelessly for the poor and disenfranchised, leaving between them at great personal expense a legacy of eleven churches, including the towering Grade I-listed Italian Gothic church of St Bartholomew's. Just as the secular architecture of Wilds and Busby had transformed Regency Brighton, the Wagners' missionary zeal for church building made a profound impact on the Victorian townscape. Out went the idealised neo-classicism of the Regency period, replaced by a pervasive Gothic revival.

With Victorianism also came industrialism, with industry came the railways, and with the railways came the masses, hot-footing it from London. When the first train steamed its way into Brighton's history books on 21 September 1841 there were those who prophesied the downfall of everything the town had become, but in truth it was just another chapter in a volume of readjustments and adaptations to circumstance. Old world wealth was replaced by mercantile and City prosperity as the commuter age beckoned. Domestic servants, artisans and clerks followed, drawn in the wake of Empire-rich industrialists, while the new locomotive works employed, at their height, over 4,000 labourers. Brighton may have been abandoned by its great royal patron, and lost some of its surface sheen, but the railways ushered in a new boom time.

By 1861 more than 250,000 visitors were descending annually on Brighton, a combination of London day-trippers drawn by relatively affordable access to the coast in the summer months, and the 'jet set' allured by a social agenda of concerts and recitals, lectures and dinner parties, hallmarks of the fashionable winter season. It was an age of great innovation: the West Pier, the Volks Railway, the world's first great aquarium; and of vigorous entrepreneurs like Eugenius Birch and Magnus Volk. It was also an age of creativity: William Thackeray wrote *Vanity Fair* in the Old Ship Hotel, and much of *Dombey and Son* was written by Charles Dickens in Brighton.

ABOVE **The Old Ship Hotel.** In the early days of Brighton's flirtation with fame and fashion, the social agenda was dominated by two coaching inns: the Castle Inn and the Old Ship. The Castle Inn was demolished in 1823 and its assembly rooms were converted by George IV into a royal chapel as part of the Pavilion estate. The interior of the chapel was later dismantled and reassembled to form St Stephen's Church in Montpelier Place (page 66). The Old Ship survived, and is now the oldest inn in Brighton. Although records only reach back to 1665, it is thought to date from the sixteenth century. It fell into the hands of the ubiquitous Nicolas Tettersell in 1671, and a century later had expanded to include a 90-foot (27-metre) ballroom. At the height of its fame, it played host to all Brighton's major social occasions – balls, concerts, town meetings, assemblies – and attracted the cream of Regency nobility. Paganini famously performed here in 1831, and both Dickens and Thackeray were regular guests.

RIGHT Sign for the Old Ship Hotel assembly rooms

TO THE OLD SHIP ASSEMBLY ROOMS FOR BALLS. BANQUETS. CONCERTS. &c.

However, as the century wore on, Brighton's schizophrenic make-up – unashamed end-of-pier populism on the one hand, the *nouveau riche* on the other – became hard to sustain. The monied classes found 'modern' Brighton rather too louche for their sensibilities, and began to sidestep the issue by relocating westwards to the sedentary but desirable environs of Hove.

This left Brighton once more on the cusp of identity crisis, and as the twentieth century dawned, it found itself caught in limbo. Pressures to reap the benefits of burgeoning mass tourism were inevitable, but as Victorianism made way for Edwardianism, Brighton seemed determined to hang on to the coat-tails of its past glories, and retain at least a simulacrum of its Regency prestige. By the 1890s artists and writers had begun to gather: Aubrey Beardsley, Roger Fry, Walter Sickert, Arnold Bennett, Oscar Wilde, Noel Coward, Ivor Novello all frequented the stucco terraces and hotel lobbies, while Rudyard Kipling and Edward Burne-Jones made their homes along the coast in nearby Rottingdean. Even Edward VII and his mistress, Lillie Langtry, patronised turn-of-the-century Brighton.

Following the First World War, which claimed the lives of over 2,500 local men but left little mark on the town itself, Brighton assumed a darker guise, emerging in the 1920s as a byword for racketeering and simmering menace, fuelled by the fiction of Graham Greene's notoriously *noir Brighton Rock* published in 1938, and the non-fiction of the infamous 1934 trunk murders. The foundations of privilege and high society fortune on which Brighton had established itself had been steadily worn away, and its role as the country's arbiter of taste and fashion was no longer tenable.

The Second World War had a far greater impact on the town. Beaches were barricaded, there was extensive air-raid damage, and as Brighton crept cautiously into the murky light of post-war Britain, its destiny hung in the balance once more.

Allotments. Brighton & Hove
boasts 6 city parks, 19 formal
gardens, 76 tennis courts,
139 recreational open
spaces and 37 allotment
sites (2,205 plots).

Since the mid-1930s its fate had lain in a political tug-of-war
between men like Herbert Carden, widely recognised as the
architect of suburban Brighton, who saw its town houses
and grand terraces as expendable anachronisms, and the
resort's proto-conservationists. Carden had seriously suggested tearing down Regency frontages in favour of high-rise
modernism. In 1945 the Regency Society was formed, its
members arguing that Brighton's future lay in the very thing
Carden and his supporters had proposed to destroy: its past.

The outcome was at best a compromise, at worst a white-
wash. For though its Georgian and Regency heritage remains
relatively intact, albeit interspersed with mid-twentieth-century
monuments to architectural pragmatism, great swathes of
Brighton's old buildings were destroyed and redeveloped in
the process.

The 1960s saw Brighton once more cultivating its taste
for hedonism, a legacy from its Regency preoccupation with
pleasure-seeking, personal liberty and a general distaste for
intervention. This also spawned an association with alternative
subcultures that has cemented its reputation ever since as one
of the most vibrant and progressive cities in the United
Kingdom. It is also an association that has spilled over into
counter-culture mythology, most famously in the beachfront
confrontations between mods and rockers that reached a
climax in the 'Battle of Brighton' over the Whitsun weekend of
17–18 May 1964. This snapshot of simmering post-war unrest
and disaffected youth culture, was revisited in 1979 in Franc
Roddam's cult classic *Quadrophenia*.

The '60s also saw Brighton politicised to a new degree. The
University of Sussex campus at Falmer, designed in utilitarian
style by Sir Basil Spence, soon gained a reputation for radical-
ism. With the birth of Brighton Festival in 1966 and a growing
art, music and culture scene, the town became a byword for
leftist bohemian chic.

Although back in the early 1930s, at the peak of the
boom, more than fifteen million people took their annual holi-
days at Britain's beach resorts, within thirty or forty years for
many resorts the writing was on the wall. What Thomas Cook
had begun back in the 1860s – the slow but steady democra-
tisation of travel – a century later translated into the first mass
package holiday exodus, as the call of the Costas beckoned
millions of Brits abroad for the first time. Like hundreds of seaside towns across the country, Brighton was forced to reinvent
itself yet again.

Where other resorts seemed to flounder in the face of seemingly irrevocable decline, Brighton had one more trick up its sleeve. The town had in fact been a conference destination of some renown since the mid-nineteenth century – the first party political conference was held by the Conservatives in 1875. But it was a century later, with the construction of the Brighton Centre and the growing status of Gatwick as the nation's second airport, that Brighton began fully to embrace the international conference market. By the late 1980s this sector was injecting an estimated £53 million into the local economy.

The boom and bust economics of the late 1980s and early '90s took their toll, however, and mass unemployment led inevitably to profound pockets of social deprivation and poverty. This is a legacy that still exists, although as the city has been steadily gentrified from the centre, its symptoms have been relegated more and more to the outlying fringes.

Throughout its history, Brighton has taken the rough with the smooth. What goes around seems inevitably to come back round again. It doesn't take a great imaginative leap of faith to trace a continuum from the heyday of the Prince Regent's reign

ABOVE Designed in Italianate style by architect David Mocatta, Brighton's railway station was built in 1841. Its recently restored iron and glass arched roof was erected in 1882–3 and spans almost 183 metres (600 feet).

ABOVE RIGHT Eric Gill's sculpture on the wall of the Brighthelm Centre, illustrating the parable of the loaves and fishes.

BELOW RIGHT Churchill Square Shopping Centre

to today's millennial boom town. The boroughs of Brighton and Hove were merged in 1997, and in 2000 the town was finally granted city status before embarking on a bold bid for European Capital of Culture 2008.

Huge investment in the nineties and noughties – from multi-million pound refurbishments of the Royal Pavilion, Dome Concert Hall, and Museum and Art Gallery to the brand new state-of-the-art Jubilee Library – have transformed not only the landscape, but Brighton's aspiration to become a city break destination to rival anywhere in Europe. And quite a transformation act it has been. Twenty-first-century Brighton has a cosmopolitan buzz about it. It is a city brimming with self-confidence and economic gravitas, a magnet for re-locators, dream seekers and lifestyle aspirants all in search of that enigmatic Brighton thing. With rocketing house prices, a rapidly changing demographic, and metropolitan expectations on a beach town infrastructure, whether Brighton can sustain its current high remains to be seen. But if history has anything to teach us, it is that this chameleon of a city was, is, and always will be ripe for reinvention.

seafront

'These well-dressed and leading people never look at the sea . . . they do not take the slightest interest . . . their pursuits are purely social and neither ladies nor gentlemen ever go on to the beach . . . the beach is ignored; it is almost, perhaps, quite vulgar . . . the sea is not the thing in Brighton.'

Richard Jeffries, *The Open Air*, 1885;
essay on 'Sunny Brighton'

At first glance, it is hard to see how Brighton's ancient Anglo-Saxon settlement, Brightelmstone, evolved and prospered on such an unforgiving stretch of coastline, open to the prevailing south-westerly gales and at the mercy of constantly advancing seas. But coastlines change. Long before the Wellesbourne, Brighton's 'lost river', was consigned underground to drain out the Steine in the late eighteenth century, it is believed that a natural harbour formed at the mouth of Pool Valley, providing a small safe haven for fishing boats. Combined with the natural windbreak of the Downs to the north and the protection of a submerged shingle bar along the beach, the prospect may not have been as bleak as might first be imagined.

Either way, prosper it did, often in spite of the sea's best laid plans, and Brighton's shifts in fortune over the centuries from medieval fishing village to 'Queen of the watering holes' are mirrored in the changing complexion of the shoreline. Though little sign remains today, Brighton's history was once defined by its fishing industry. First mentioned in the Domesday Survey of 1086, Brightelmstone's embryonic fishing community grew up on the extensive foreshore below the crumbling chalk cliff. As the settlement increased, the Lower Town community expanded on to the cliff-top above, and formed today's Old Town. Hemp was

RIGHT **Bathers, West Pier**

BELOW **View from Lewes Crescent – a lone fishing boat returns home.**

RIGHT **Lobster/crab pots at Brighton Marina**

BELOW RIGHT **Shelling cockles outside Brighton's Fishing Museum**

ABOVE Fishing fleet at Brighton Marina

LEFT Outside Brighton Fishing Museum

OVERLEAF Brighton Pier at dusk

grown for rope in the old Hempshares (now the Lanes), and flax for sails in neighbouring Hove.

A colony of Flemings settled in the Old Town in the thirteenth century, contributing substantially to the growth of the fishing community, and by the 1580s Brighton's sizeable fleet was setting sail for 'fares' as far afield as Scarborough in Yorkshire and Yarmouth in Norfolk. By the mid-1600s Brighton was arguably the most significant fishery in Sussex, with a population approaching four thousand.

Prosperity, however, was short lived. With rising seas, and a rapidly eroding foreshore, by the time of the economic slump of the 1640s Brighton was already facing a precipitous decline. Daniel Defoe, after a fleeting visit, remarked in his *Tour Through the Whole Island of Great Britain* that 'the sea is very unkind', and that Brighton's inhabitants 'might reasonably expect it would eat up the whole town'. Petitions were made for emergency sea defences to prevent just such a fate, but the

call went unheeded, and the great storms of 1703 and 1705 finally put paid to the Lower Town. By this time, the fishing fleet had been reduced to just twenty-five boats.

For many, including Defoe, who professed that the cost of sea defences would be more than the whole town was worth, Brighton's future was untenable. Nevertheless, with charitable funds raised through national 'Church Briefs' (letters patent issued by the Crown and read out in all churches in a certain area in favour of petitioners whose needs were urgent), Brighton's first groynes were erected in 1724, a pattern of construction that continued throughout the eighteenth and nineteenth centuries, halting erosion and transforming the geography of its shoreline.

It was a physician, however, that made the most immediate impact on the face of Brighton's coastline. Dr Richard Russell published his *Dissertation Concerning the Use of Sea Water in Diseases of the Glands* in Latin in 1750, and in English three

FAR LEFT **The Regency Fish Restaurant**

LEFT **Regency Square**

RIGHT **Looking east towards Brighton Pier**

years later. The efficacies of seawater quickly attracted the monied classes, and changed the town's demography as assisted bathing from large, purpose-built, wooden bathing machines became the *de rigueur* pastime. Brighton's foreshore was no longer the sole domain of fishermen.

The influx of wealthy visitors led inevitably to a conflict between the rights of the fishing community and the steady march towards gentrification. The Steine, where the fishermen and women traditionally dried their nets and hauled their boats up from the sea, was 'cleaned up' and transformed into a fashionable promenade ground. The cliff-top capstans were dismantled and the fishermen were forced to share the fore-shore with the first front of Brighton's fledgling tourist boom.

A number of enterprising fishermen and women, including the redoubtable Martha Gunn, the Queen of Brighton's 'dip-pers', and the Prince of Wales' own personal assistant, John 'Smoaker' Miles, saw the writing on the wall, and reinvented themselves as professional 'bathers', vigorously plunging their clients in and out of the waves for a modest living.

For the late eighteenth-century visitor, drawn purely by its restorative charms, Brighton's working seafront held little romantic association and was in fact considered a rather unruly aspect. As detailed in *The New Brighton Guide* of 1796, satirist and journalist Anthony Pasquin (aka John Williams) thought Brighton's coast 'like the greater part of its visitors, bold, saucy, intrusive and dangerous'. The new seafront crescents and terraces of the Steine cast a discerning gaze over this working scene: passengers being rowed ashore or unceremoniously ferried on the bent backs of fishermen through the surf from sailing packets arriving from Dieppe; coal brigs unloading their dusty cargos; bathers taking their morning constitutionals.

These scenes were preserved for posterity in early nineteenth-century paintings of J.M.W. Turner and John Constable, and a century later by Walter Sickert and Spencer Gore. It is through Constable, in a famous letter to his friend Archdeacon John Fisher in 1824 (Beckett, 1968), that we get one of the most evocative portraits of Brighton's Regency beachfront:

'. . . the beach is only Piccadilly by the sea-side. Ladies dressed & *undressed* – Gentlemen in morning gowns & slippers on or without them altogether about knee-deep in the breakers – footmen – children – nursery maids. dogs. boys. fishermen – *preventive service men* (with hangers and pistols). rotten fish & those amphibious animals the old bathing women, whose language both in oaths and voice resembles men – all are mixed together in endless & indecent confusion . . . in short there is nothing here for a painter but the breakers – & sky.'

Although the steady decline in fishing continued unabated (150 fishing boats in 1862, 88 in 1902, and only 48 by 1948), Brighton's fishermen continued to land their distinctive wide-beamed hog boats or 'hoggies' on the beachfront, where they sold their seasonal catches by Dutch auction (in which the auctioneer starts at a high price and reduces until sale made) at the makeshift fish market beneath the low cliffs.

OPPOSITE ABOVE Day trippers, immediately east of Brighton Pier

OPPOSITE BELOW Beach huts on Hove front

BELOW Beach from Brighton Pier looking west

The beachfront itself continued to change shape. As the town extended east and westwards from the centre, further sea defences were erected and more and more of the foreshore was reclaimed and redeveloped to create Madeira Lawns, the Lower Esplanade and King's Road Arches. The crumbling east cliffs were shored up, first with a simple flint structure in the early 1800s and then with a vast cement wall that eventually ran from the Steine right through to Kemp Town in the 1830s. Similar construction began to transform the contours of the town's western beachfront, initially from Ship Street to Black Lion Street, and eventually out from the Grand Hotel to the border with Hove in 1894.

With the end of the Napoleonic Wars in 1815, Brighton's fame spread and it became necessary to find a more appropriate means of accommodating the inevitable upsurge in cross-Channel traffic. As there was no natural harbour, the only viable solution was to extend out into the sea, and in September 1823, at a cost of £30,000, the 350-metre (1148-foot) long Chain Pier was opened to much fanfare. Although, there was a distinct lack of royal patronage, one of the backers was the influential local landowner George Wyndham, 3rd Earl of Egremont. The pier, a feat of engineering, was also an aesthetic triumph, a defining perpendicular brush stroke on an otherwise unremarkable horizontal canvas of sea and endless sky, as recorded by Turner for his patron, Lord Egremont. Though primarily an embarkation point, the Chain Pier soon attracted promenaders, and with the addition of a bazaar, saloon lounge, reading room and *camera obscura*, became the world's first pleasure pier. Competition from the West Pier, built in 1866 by Eugenius Birch for the express purpose of promenading,

made short shrift of Brighton's first Iron Lady, though the sea had the final say, dragging the ailing structure asunder in the storms of 1896.

So began the brief reign of the West Pier, Queen of the pleasure piers and arguably the most elegant seafront construction ever built (it is one of only two UK piers with a Grade I listing). With its delicate filigree ironwork and oriental-style pavilion, the West Pier was the quintessential Victorian vision of the pleasure promenade. In its glory days Charlie Chaplin, Stan Laurel, Rex Harrison and Ralph Richardson performed to packed houses from its waterfront theatre-cum-concert hall.

However, with the arrival of the Palace Pier in 1899 – the last of Brighton's great Victorian engineering endeavours – came a credible contender for the West Pier's crown. At the peak of its pre-war fame in 1939, its theatre, bandstand and large winter garden attracted two million visitors, including forty-five thousand on a single Bank Holiday Monday.

For the last quarter of a century, the West Pier has been plagued by disaster, helped along the road to ruin by storm damage, arson and bureaucratic intransigence. Today all that remains is a rusting carcass, a skeletal impression of its former glory, and a scourge on the city's conscience. In contrast, the Palace Pier (renamed Brighton Pier in 2000) remains, over a century after its triumphant opening, one of the top tourist attractions in the country, drawing more than 4.5 million visitors every year.

Another great act of entrepreneurial Victorian vigour was Magnus Volk's Electric Railway, the first construction of its type in Britain, built in 1883. Son of a German immigrant clockmaker, Volk also established the first telephone line in Brighton and

LEFT **Helter-skelter, Brighton Pier.** In Graham Greene's 1938 novel *Brighton Rock*, the notorious gang leader Pinkie Brown plunges to his death from the pier. Earlier in the novel he murders Fred Hale, masquerading as Kolley Kibber, on the ghost train.

ABOVE **Magnus Volk's Electric Railway, built in 1883**

ABOVE RIGHT **Grand Junction roundabout, looking south towards the head of Brighton Pier**

BELOW RIGHT **Pink sky over Pink Pride festivities**

fitted the Royal Pavilion with electric lights. Almost a century and a quarter after its maiden voyage, the Volk's Railway still trundles along its 1.1 miles of track from the Sea Life Centre to Black Rock. Volk's most ambitious undertaking was the ill-fated Brighton and Rottingdean Seashore Electric Railway opened in 1896. Rumoured to have inspired H.G. Wells' *War of the Worlds*, and appropriately nicknamed Daddy Long Legs, the two-tiered saloon car ferried passengers along a 3-mile track above the sea, propped up on four legs 7 metres (23 feet) in length. At high tide the track itself was submerged by up to 5 metres (16 feet) of water. Not surprisingly, only five years after its inaugural run, it made its final waterlogged excursion.

The seafront was further transformed by the arrival of the Grand Hotel (1869) and the Metropole (1890) whose imposing façades dwarfed the traditional seafront hostelries such as the Old Ship and the Royal Albion, which had played such a key role in the town's first great leap of faith towards celebrity.

By the mid-nineteenth century, Brighton's seafront had become a mass of contradictions. On the one hand, it was a summer playground for day-trippers spilling off the London trains down to the beach. On the other, it provided a short sharp winter season for the fashionable elite in the front's exclusive terraces and hotels. And, of course, there were the fishermen, fighting a losing battle with the steady march of progress.

With the widening of the King's Road in 1864–65, the fishermen, who had traditionally stored their gear in huts beneath the cliff-top, were further displaced. For close on another century there were still full-timers launching from the beach, but the closure of the traditional marketplace in 1960 and pressures of mass tourism sealed the fate of Brighton's beachfront fishing industry. The last stragglers relocated to Shoreham, Newhaven and the eastern end of Brighton Marina in the 1970s.

Though today fishing vessels no longer set sail from Brighton's beaches, fishing remains a viable, if marginalised

ABOVE **Brighton Pier**

RIGHT **Bathers, Brighton Pier**

industry. Despite ever more complex red tape over catch quotas and net sizes, and universally depleted stocks, local fishermen continue to trawl with state-of-the-art GPS (Global Positioning System) and twenty-first-century fish-finding technologies. In recent years freshly landed fish has begun to be sold once more beneath the King's Road Arches.

The twentieth century wrought further reconstruction on the front with new high-rise modernist developments, such as the recently renovated Embassy Court (1935) butted up against Georgian antiquity. Permanent tourist amenities were provided, and the commercial development of the esplanade took on new momentum.

At 5pm on 2 July 1940, Brighton's coastline was closed off, its beaches mined and strung up with barbed wire, not to reopen for another five years. At the end of the Second World War the town's fishermen, returning from service in the Merchant and Royal Navies, took once more to the helms of paddle steamers, sailing boats and deep-sea angling charters for Brighton's growing tourist trade.

The love affair of the 1960s and 1970s with concrete and lax planning law gave birth to a number of incongruous monoliths, including the 126-acre Brighton Marina at Black Rock, the largest undertaking of its kind in the country. It finally provided the city with the harbour it had hankered after for centuries, but remains for many a controversial example of lacklustre ambition and missed opportunity.

Today Brighton's beachfront is an aggregation of old and new, a mix of kiss-me-quick seaside frivolity and laid-back surf culture insouciance. Depending on the trick of the light, it could be San Francisco with deckchairs and beach huts, or Margate with Venice Beach aspirations. Its fishermen's arches are now artist's studios, its esplanade given over to volleyball, wireless internet and endless yardage of chrome table-tops and beach-bar umbrellas. By day it is still the haunt of fish-smokers and fortune-tellers. By night it is a hedonist's playground as club-land opens its doors and spills out on to the water's edge in a twenty-first-century homage to the great Regency aesthetic: the unashamed pursuit of pleasure.

BELOW Annual scooter run, Madeira Drive. Brighton mod culture was immortalised in Franc Roddam's 1979 movie *Quadrophenia*.

RIGHT The distinctive black façade of Royal Crescent was the first development to be built facing the sea. These timber-framed houses date from 1798 and were hung with glazed 'mathematical' tiles designed to resemble a brick construction.

BELOW RIGHT Boer War Memorial, Royal Sussex Regiment

BELOW Brighton's Victorian sewers are a fine example of nineteenth-century ingenuity and modern technology. Completed in 1874 at a cost of £104,608, they still form the backbone of Brighton & Hove's sewerage system today.

LEFT AND TOP RIGHT Like a sleek modernist ocean liner, Embassy Court first sailed into view in 1936, bringing in its wake a tidal wave of change that at one point threatened to engulf Brighton's Regency skyline. It was designed by Wells Coates, who was influenced by arch-modernist Le Corbusier, the Expressionist architecture of Erich Mendelssohn, and Japanese culture and design. The modernist creed was 'form follows function' – a far cry from the Regency aesthetic – and Embassy Court was the first purpose-built development in England to boast penthouses and sunrooms. After years of neglect, it has recently been whipped into shipshape form courtesy of a new facelift from Conran & Partners.

RIGHT The vast Italianate Grand Hotel, built in 1862–4, has 30 miles of flooring and 6 miles of gas piping. Over the years it has played host to such esteemed guests as Napoleon III, Winston Churchill and J.F. Kennedy. It survived an infamous bombing, when the IRA tried to assassinate Margaret Thatcher during a Conservative Party conference on 12 October 1984.

kemp town

'Kemp Town is too charming; it is a little kingdom of one's own.'

Lady Granville, 1832

Strictly speaking Kemp Town is the grand, Grade I-listed Regency estate at the eastern extremity of Brighton, made up of the imposing classical façades of Arundel and Chichester Terraces, the monumental sweep of Lewes Crescent, and the elegant mansion houses of Sussex Square.

But today its boundaries are less clearly defined, and the name Kemp Town can be loosely applied to everything east of the Steine through to Black Rock. Sporting an air of maverick eccentricity, modern Kemp Town is Brighton at its most offbeat and streetwise. Its vitality and colour derive in part from its flourishing gay community, but also from its refusal to conform to twenty-first-century notions of town planning. It is a city quarter with a distinctly village sensibility. Its main thoroughfare – St James's Street leading into St George's Road – has somehow sidestepped the tyranny of chain culture, and retains a stubborn streak of independence. Its public houses, bars, cafés, delis, health food shops, flea markets, barbers, fishmongers, and beauty parlours (for men) share an idiosyncratic charm and are housed in a loose affiliation of nineteenth-century bow-fronted shop fronts, interrupted by small squares and side streets of B&Bs leading down to the sea.

The estate itself was a bold and extravagant speculation, dreamed up by Thomas Read Kemp – political radical, religious dissenter, Member of Parliament for Lewes and leading citizen of Brighton – on the cusp of the great 1820s property boom. At the time, Brighton's eastern extent ran as far as Royal Crescent, an isolated resort development (the first of its kind to be built facing the sea) constructed on the East Cliff for

RIGHT **St James's Street**

West Indian merchant J.B. Otto in 1789. Beyond this was open land right up to the edge of the Downs and the racecourse, most of which was owned by Kemp himself. The Old Town was cramped and ill equipped to cater for Brighton's new breed of visitor, and the Steine was rapidly becoming oversubscribed. Kemp's plan was conceived as a self-contained out-of-town sanctuary, complete with hotel, church and mews cottages, where Regency Society could retreat from the hubbub in relative seclusion.

To realise his vision, Kemp employed the services of architects Charles Augustin Busby and Amon Henry Wilds, and work began in earnest in May 1823. It has often been assumed that it was Amon Wilds Senior who formed the prolific architectural partnership with Busby. Recent evidence, however, suggests that it was in fact his son of the same name who set up practice in Hanover Crescent with political activist, liberal reformer and budding young London architect Busby. The catalyst for this partnership was no doubt Kemp himself, who had employed the Wilds family on previous developments, but felt that such a vast undertaking required the wider experience of Busby.

Loosely based on John Nash's stuccoed terraces for London's Regent's Park, Kemp Town was a hugely ambitious piece of grand theatre, an Olympian stage-set in classical revivalist style replete with Doric porches and Corinthian pilasters, and set off by landscaped private enclosures overlooking the sea. The scale was unprecedented, Lewes Crescent spanning some 250 metres (820 feet), 60 metres (200 feet) wider than Bath's Royal Crescent, and the design was unique in its bold synthesis of forms.

As with many such developments, its 106 houses (a fraction of Busby's original scheme) were designed and built as grand-fronted skeletons to be fleshed out by speculators and individual purchasers such as master builder and entrepreneur Thomas Cubitt, who built thirty-seven of Kemp Town's grand mansions. Consequently each house is unique in its internal layout and design.

The four acres of private gardens were enclosed in 1823 and laid out four years later by the botanist Henry Phillips, who was also the originator of the ill-fated Anthaeum (see page107). His scheme included a tunnel running under what

ABOVE **The late-Victorian Madeira Lift on Marine Parade is a listed building decorated with four dragons and an ornate dolphin weather-vane.**

LEFT Victoria Fountain, Old Steine. The Old Steine takes its name from a Flemish word meaning stone. During excavations in 1823 large sarsen stones – natural sandstone blocks worn smooth by the last period of glaciation – were discovered. They now form the base of the Victoria Fountain, designed by A.H. Wilds in 1846 for the Queen's twenty-seventh birthday.

BELOW LEFT The Old Steine

BELOW Lewes Crescent

LEFT **New Steine**

BELOW LEFT **Cobble-fronted houses on the Old Steine**

BELOW **Centurions caught off guard on St James's Street during the annual Pride celebrations, one of the biggest free gay and lesbian festivals in Britain.**

LEFT The distinctive pagoda roof of the Hanbury Arms Ballroom once concealed the remains of Sir Albert Sassoon, Anglo-Indian philanthropist, and descendant of Jewish merchants from Baghdad. Built in 1892 as a mausoleum for the Sassoon family – known as the 'Rothschilds of the East' – the building was later used as an air-raid shelter during the Second World War. Today it is part of the adjacent Hanbury Arms, and the heartland of Kemp Town's alternative club scene. Beneath its domed ceiling is a sensualist's playground of laptop dj-ing sessions, Japanese Manga screenings, occult festivals and full-on fetish nights.

BEOW LEFT **Camelford Street –** these late eighteenth- and early nineteenth-century cottages are some of the oldest surviving houses in the city outside of the Old Town.

BELOW RIGHT **Margaret Street**

is now Marine Parade, and private cottages for the resident gardener and constable. The latter had dispensation to admit non-residents as long as they were suitably dressed. Tennis courts and croquet lawn were added in the late 1880s. The Kemp Town esplanade and slopes, running down from the tunnel entrance below Marine Parade to the beach were landscaped by William Kendall between 1828 and 1830, with the addition of a reading room in 1835. During the Second World War the gardens were appropriated by the military, the tunnel bricked over and the wrought-iron railings requisitioned for the war effort.

Marine Parade itself – a defining architectural statement of the Regency period, and perhaps the finest seafront façade in the country – is lined with many of its grandest developments: Royal Crescent, Lewes Crescent, Chichester Terrace, Marine Square. Constructed between 1790 and 1850, it ran from the

Steine eastwards to the Kemp Town estate, and was shored up against the sea by a vast wall. It soon became a fashionable promenade route for horse-drawn carriages and equestrians between Kemp Town and Brunswick. The ornately decorated Madeira Lift – now a listed building – was opened in May 1890 and descended to the latticed arches of Madeira Terrace and Madeira Drive below. In 1908, in honour of Edward VII, Marine Parade was officially renamed King's Cliff. Though every effort was made by the council to encourage its wider use to cover the whole of the Kemp Town ward, the name never stuck.

Owing to its isolated position, the Kemp Town estate was not an immediate success. In 1828 only eleven houses were occupied, and dozens remained incomplete and untenanted for several decades, leaving Kemp, who had invested much of his vast fortune in its construction, so over-

ABOVE **Portland Place. These symmetrical terraces were the last works in Brighton designed by Charles Busby.**

ABOVE RIGHT **Marine Parade**

stretched that he was forced to withdraw from public life and leave the country in 1837. He died in relative obscurity in Paris in 1844, aged sixty-two, the same year that a proclamation of outlawry against him was nailed to the door of St Nicholas Church by one of his many creditors.

A horse-drawn bus service to Brighton station from 1840 substantially improved Kemp Town's prospects. As an article published in 1846 in the *Brighton Herald* reported: 'Kemp Town is evidently in the ascendant, and from the vast number of the aristocracy, and those including lots of titled personages, who congregate there, it is no longer doubtful that it will soon eclipse every other part of our favourite town.'

Throughout its history, it has indeed attracted the well-heeled and well-connected. Kemp himself lived at 22 Sussex Square from 1827 and Thomas Cubitt took up permanent residence at 13 Lewes Crescent in 1846. William IV and Queen

Adelaide, and later Victoria and Albert frequented Kemp Town's private enclosures, and in February 1908, Edward VII, during a visit to his daughter Princess Louise, Duchess of Fife, secured the enclosures for his own private use.

William Cavendish, 6th Duke of Devonshire (after whom Duke's Mound was named) purchased 1 Lewes Crescent and the adjacent 14 Chichester Terrace in 1828/9, from which he played host to an impressive gallery of house guests that included William IV and Queen Adelaide, the Duke and Duchess of Cumberland (later King and Queen of Hanover), the Prince and Princess of Parma, and the exiled Austrian Chancellor, Prince Metternich. In later years the two houses were taken by the Duke and Duchess of Fife, who continued to entertain in similar vein, rounding off the list of distinguished visitors with five kings, four queens and most of Europe's exiled nobility.

LEFT **Kemp Town enclosures**

OPPOSITE LEFT **Belgrave Place, Marine Parade**

OPPOSITE TOP RIGHT
Kemp Town enclosures. Popular local mythology holds that the Rev. Charles Lutwidge Dodgson (aka Lewis Carroll) wrote his classic children's fantasy *Alice's Adventures in Wonderland* at 11 Sussex Square, and was inspired by this ivy-strewn tunnel. However, as *Alice* was published in 1865, a decade before Carroll's Brighton residency (he stayed here on and off between 1874 and 1887), this charming slice of Brighton folklore is almost certainly apocryphal.

OPPOSITE BOTTOM RIGHT
Belgrave Place, Marine Parade

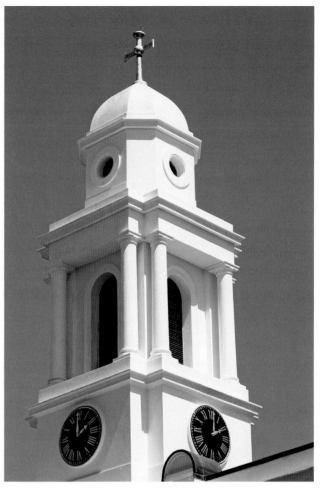

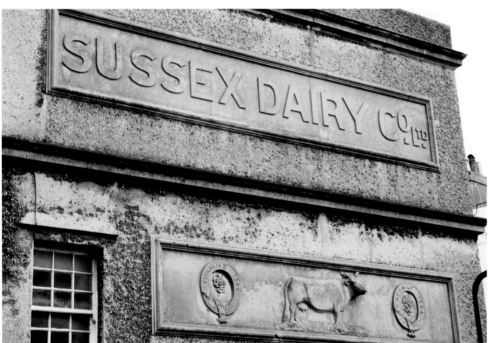

TOP Brighton College. This rather forbidding flint-fronted Gothic public school for boys was built in 1848/9 by Sir George Gilbert Scott. Its express purpose was to provide 'a thoroughly liberal and practical education in conformity with the principles of the established Church'. It went co-educational in 1988.

Among its former alumni are the Antarctic explorer Sir Vivian Fuchs, actor Sir Michael Hordern and comedian/writer Tony Hawks.

ABOVE RIGHT St George's Chapel, built in 1824 by Charles Augustin Busby for Thomas Kemp's new estate, is one of Brighton's most elegant neo-classical Regency buildings, complete with recessed Ionic pilasters and a gleaming white Grecian bell tower. William IV's consort Queen Adelaide was a frequent worshipper throughout the 1830s.

ABOVE Cow Corner, St George's Road

ABOVE **The Church of St John
the Baptist**

LEFT **The Church of St John
the Baptist. Mrs Fitzherbert
outlived George IV, dying in
1837 at the ripe age of eighty.
She is buried near the altar
of St John the Baptist Church,
mother church to Brighton's
Roman Catholics. A memorial
by John Edward Carew shows
a kneeling Maria Fitzherbert
wearing three rings on her
wedding finger, a bold visual
reminder of her ill-fated royal
alliance.**

From 1869 until 1931 the estate was also serviced by
its own railway line, built at vast expense with the principal
intention of preventing the construction of a rival line into East
Brighton. No mean feat of engineering, the line was a huge
undertaking, straddling two viaducts and a vast tunnel beneath
the chalk cliffs of Race Hill. However, it had a truncated life-
span. Because it could not compete with the bus companies,
the passenger service was withdrawn in 1932, and from then
until final closure in 1971 the railway served as a goods line
only. The tunnel functioned as an air-raid shelter during the war,
and today part of its extent is used as a mushroom farm.

Over the years writers and novelists – from Lewis Carroll
and William Harrison Ainsworth to Anthony Dale have either
visited or made Kemp Town enclosures their home. In her book
Pepita, poet and novelist Vita Sackville-West gives a vivid
account of the extravagant transformation of the interior of
39–40 Sussex Square by her mother, Lady Sackville, and the

architect Sir Edwin Lutyens in the 1920s. Inevitably, the house
– and along with it the Sackville interior – has long since gone
the way of most of Brighton's great Regency developments,
subdivided into flats in the post-war period as economic
exigency dictated. Indeed, in the late 1940s the estate had
fallen into such disrepair and mismanagement that its entire
value was estimated at less than £250,000, and whole houses
in Lewes Crescent could be snapped up for £2,000.

Today things have gone full circle. The Kemp Town estate
is again one of the city's most desirable neighbourhoods,
patronised by today's equivalent of Regency celebrity, as movie
stars and media millionaires buy into a modern interpretation of
Kemp's nineteenth-century vision. Meanwhile contemporary
Kemp Town itself performs a fine balancing act between its
own delightfully camp brand of Bohemia and an inevitable
creep towards gentrification.

montpelier, clifton hill and st nicholas church

Within a whisker of the city's throng lies a remarkably well-preserved reminder of Brighton's affluent past. Poised above the city and casting a regal gaze out across the sea, the Montpelier and Clifton Hill district is home to some of Brighton's most elegant architecture. This outstanding conservation area grew up north of Western Road, and west of Dyke Road to the Hove border. It was developed between the 1820s and 1860s, spawned by the town's first great property boom and later capitalising on the arrival of the railway in 1841. Everything west of the new terminus became hot property as the wealthy middle classes migrated upwind of the smoke, above the 'unwholesome' air of the fishermen's quarter, and out towards the rarefied sanctity of Hove.

The name Montpelier derives from the French Mediterranean city of Montpellier, seat of an ancient university, and a favoured destination for seventeenth- and early eighteenth-century British aristocrats on the Grand Tour of Europe. Due to its elevated position, temperate climate and malaria-free air, it gained a reputation as a major cultural resort for the leisured classes. The name thus began to appear in fashionable resort towns across England, becoming synonymous with the most sought-after districts, which were invariably of high elevation, mild climate and pleasing panorama. In short, Montpellier (or Montpelier) was a byword for 'the most favoured spot', and towns like Cheltenham, York or indeed Brighton could lay claim to the title 'Montpellier of England'.

RIGHT The semi-detached Italianate Montpelier Villas were designed in late Regency style in 1845 by A.H. Wilds and built on the site of a bluebell wood. The romance of this may perhaps have been lost on one-time occupant Gilbert Harding, radio broadcaster and professional curmudgeon, who was once described as 'the rudest man in Britain'.

LEFT **Bluebells in Montpelier Villas**

BELOW **Upper North Street**

RIGHT **This flint wall once kept the cows from trespassing on Thomas Kemp's eccentric residence, The Temple.**

FAR RIGHT **Thomas Read Kemp's dome-roofed villa was said to have been modelled on the Temple of Solomon. After much alteration, it is now Brighton & Hove High School for Girls.**

Dr Wigan's 1834 treatise *Brighton and Its Three Climates* makes just such a claim for the town's own Montpelier district, believing the area to be 'the most salubrious in Brighton', and remarking, with alarming optimism, that 'many invalids . . . have recovered immediately when sent to the top of Montpelier Road or Montpelier Terrace.' Whatever the truth of this, Brighton's Montpelier became a highly desirable area for well-heeled convalescents and the new middle classes – doctors, solicitors, retired military and entrepreneurs. The area flourished, and Regency-style terraces of three and four-storey town-houses – many recorded as single occupancy at the time – sprang up in response to consumer demand. In 1851 nearly 200 of its finer houses – from the Italianate bow-fronted Montpelier Villas to the elegant curve of Montpelier Crescent – were functioning as private schools, catering for over four thousand pupils. Many houses bore the hallmarks of the town's pre-eminent architectural partnership, Amon Henry Wilds and Charles Augustin Busby.

Not surprisingly, the district attracted many of the town's most significant figures. Among them were the Rev. Henry Wagner, the Mayor of Brighton (over the years a number of Brighton mayors have been incumbent at Montpelier Hall), and Thomas Read Kemp, whose suitably eccentric residence, The Temple, was thought to be fashioned by A. & A.H. Wilds on the Temple of Solomon. Replete with Egyptian columns,

domed roof and towering corner chimneys, it was built at a cost of £15,000, and christened 'Kemp's Folly' by local sceptics. Kemp lived here in virtual isolation until 1827, while embarking on the ambitious estate that bears his name on the eastern outskirts of the town. After much alteration, it is now home to Brighton & Hove High School for Girls.

One of the area's landmark developments of the period is the exquisite Clifton Terrace. Completed in 1847 with distinctive canopied bays and fine aspect, it was one of the last great housing developments to be constructed in the grand Regency style. It was financed by the Baring family, founders of that imperial monolith, Barings Bank, and related to Kemp through his first marriage. Its secluded private gardens, laid out across the road in front of the terrace, were built on the original site of Clifton Windmill, which was moved to Windmill Street in the late 1830s.

Another striking architectural statement was Montpelier Crescent, built by Amon Henry Wilds between 1843 and 1847 on the site of Lee's Trap Cricket ground (otherwise known as Lilywhites or Temple Fields) where Sussex famously played All England in 1842. Widely considered to be Wilds' finest accomplishment, its dramatic sweep bears some of the best preserved examples of the family's architectural calling card: distinctive spiral ammonite capitals and volutes of scallop shells. The origins of the 'ammonite order' of architecture

RIGHT **Clifton Place**

BELOW RIGHT **Powis Square** is one of the very few enclosed inland squares in Brighton. Its distinctive K-6 type red telephone boxes are now listed buildings in their own right.

BELOW These spiral ammonite capitals were the calling card of Brighton's pre-eminent architectural family, Amon and Amon Henry Wilds.

TOP **Montpelier Place**

ABOVE **Port Hall**, an early nineteenth-century house and folly said to have been haunted by the ghost of a red Crusader.

RIGHT **Victoria Road**

OPPOSITE ABOVE **Guildford Street**

OPPOSITE BELOW **Powis Villas**, built in the early 1850s

ABOVE LEFT St Stephen's Hall began life in the late eighteenth century as the ballroom of Brighton's celebrated Castle Inn. The ballroom was bought by George IV and turned into a royal chapel in 1823. Thirty years later, the chapel was in turn taken down, moved a mile across the city and reassembled as St Stephen's Church. Semi-retired, this faded beauty is currently paying her debt to society dishing out square meals and sound advice to the homeless.

BELOW LEFT An early nineteenth-century coach house on Clifton Hill.

ABOVE LEFT Borough Street marks the creation of the Parliamentary Borough of Brighton in 1832.

ABOVE RIGHT Montpelier Crescent

lie with the eighteenth-century portrait painter and architect George Dance the Younger, who first employed the idea for Boydell's Gallery (Shakespeare's Gallery) in London's Pall Mall in 1789. The influence stems from an Enlightenment preoccupation with natural sciences, of which geology was by far the most prevalent discipline, informing nineteenth-century biology and setting the stage for Charles Darwin's *Origin of Species* in 1859.

Though the punning allusion to their shared Christian name (Amon) was undoubtedly a factor in the Wilds' adoption of the ammonite order, this choice of natural over geometric forms in art and architecture also reflects a sea change in early nineteenth-century thinking. Appropriately, this signature flourish was first seen in the Wilds' designs for Castle Place in Lewes, home of renowned geologist Gideon Mantell. Further ammonite examples in Brighton can be found at Hanover Crescent, Montpelier Road, Oriental Place, Richmond Terrace and Western Terrace.

Like much of Brighton, Montpelier and Clifton Hill also has an eclectic literary provenance. In Graham Greene's *Brighton*

ABOVE The fourteenth-century bell tower of Brighton's ancient parish church of St Nicholas.

LEFT The Norman font, *c.* 1170, of St Nicholas Church. This is probably the finest piece of Norman carving in Sussex.

RIGHT St Nicholas Church

FAR RIGHT Lady Chapel, St Nicholas Church

Rock, Pinkie Brown and fellow hoodlums board in Montpelier Road. In Charles Dickens' *Dombey and Son*, Paul Dombey attended Dr Blimber's School in Brighton, thought to be based on a property in Hampton Place. *The Blotting Book*, by E.F. Benson (of *Mapp and Lucia* fame) finds its solicitor hero ensconced in a 'comfortable home in Montpelier Road'. Playwright Alan Melville was also a resident of Clifton Terrace and later Victoria Street.

St Nicholas Church

Long before Clifton Hill began to flourish as a desirable postcode for the post-Regency middle classes, the flint-faced fourteenth-century church of St Nicholas stood sentinel on a bare hill overlooking the Old Town. It was dedicated to the patron saint of fishermen and protected by its elevation from the relentless attrition of the sea and the ever-present threat of attack from across the Channel. Though evidence of an even earlier church is cited in the Domesday Book, St Nicholas was

Brighton's original parish church, serving a growing congregation until it lost its tenure to Charles Barry's Gothic Revival Church of St Peter's in 1873.

Immune to the ravages of both ocean and invasion for close on 400 years it failed, however, to see off the excesses of nineteenth-century architectural ambition. Early expansion saw additional galleries built to accommodate the town's poorer worshippers, mainly fishermen from the Old Town, while the pews were rented to the growing number of wealthy penitents. Commissioned by the Rev. Henry Wagner in 1853 to further expand and restore the church in the wake of the town's Victorian population explosion, Richard Cromwell Carpenter set about a virtual rebuild, and all that remains today of the original mediaeval construction are the flint tower, chancel arch and nave arcade. Ironically Carpenter actually managed to reduce the building's capacity from 1,300 to 900 in the process, which proved insufficient to warrant its continued status as parish church.

LEFT St Michael and
All Angels Church

BELOW Lady Chapel,
St Michael and All Angels
Church

RIGHT St Michael and
All Angels Church contains
the finest collection of
Pre-Raphaelite stained glass
in Europe.

Inside there is a memorial cross to one of St Nicholas's more celebrated worshippers, the Duke of Wellington, who had died a year prior to restoration in 1852, and memorial tablets to Dr Samuel Johnson and Thomas Read Kemp. The church's most prized possession, however, is its fabulous Norman font, thought to date from the early twelfth century, carved from a single block of Caen stone. Outside is a mediaeval cross that purportedly signifies the site of a plague pit dating from 1348, the year of the Black Death.

The graveyard of St Nicholas reads like a *Who's Who* of Brighton's great and good, providing the final resting places of Captain Nicolas Tettersell (whose ship carried Charles II to safety following his famous flight from Worcester), Sake Dene Mahomed (the man who introduced Turkish baths to England, and later became 'shampooing surgeon' to George IV), Martha Gunn (Brighton's most famous bathing dipper) and the truly remarkable Phoebe Hessel.

Phoebe Hessel's picaresque tale has become the stuff of Brighton folklore. It is also a perfect symbol of a town enamoured by the art of masquerade. Born Phoebe Smith in London's Limehouse in 1713, Hessel fell in love with a soldier whom she followed all the way to the West Indies, disguised as a young infantryman. She kept up her charade for a remarkable seventeen years, and her true identity was only discovered after she was injured at the Battle of Fontenoy in Flanders in 1745. Subsequently discharged from military service, she was finally able to marry her beau. She survived two husbands and lived to the venerable age of 108, living out her days hawking her wares on the corner of the Steine and Marine Parade until pensioned off by the Prince of Wales to the tune of half a guinea a week.

St Michael's and All Angels Church

Described as the 'cathedral of the backstreets in the heart of the city', and included among the foremost one hundred in Simon Jenkins' *England's Thousand Best Churches*, the Grade I-listed St Michael's and All Angels is in fact two churches in one.

The original building, designed in Gothic Revival style in 1858 by G.F. Bodley and built in 1861–2, was the first brick-built church in Brighton. No sooner was it complete, however, than plans were mooted for its enlargement to accommodate the growing Montpelier congregation. In 1895, some thirty years after William Burges' designs for the extension were submitted, the north aisle of the original church was pulled down and the new building grafted on to its side. In essence Bodley's original construction became the south aisle and side chapel of a far larger church.

Though from the outside this incongruous red-brick, High Victorian Gothic hybrid stands somewhat at odds with the distinctive white stucco terraces of Montpelier, inside is another

story altogether. The old church is an exercise in intimate detailing, with ecclesiastical stained-glass work by the recently established firm of Morris & Co., using the designs of Pre-Raphaelite masters Edward Burne-Jones, Ford Maddox Brown and William Morris himself, textiles and ironwork by Charles Eamer Kempe, and a sixteenth-century Flemish reredos. In contrast, the soaring, vaulted thirteenth-century style French Gothic nave of the new church resonates with all the grandeur of a scaled-down Amiens or Chartres.

the cultural quarter, royal pavilion and north laine

'The Pavilion, cost a million,
As a monument to Art.
And the wits here, say it sits here,
Like an Oriental tart.'

   Noel Coward, *Conversation Piece*, 1934

William Hazlitt thought it an incongruous collection of stone pumpkins and pepper boxes. William Cobbett likened it to an upturned box of turnips and hyacinth bulbs. Perhaps most famously, Sydney Smith thought that 'the dome of St Paul's must have come down to Brighton and pupped!' Triumphant monument to exoticism or uber-kitsch princely folly? However you look at it, the Royal Pavilion will always be both the symbolic and physical heart of Brighton.

   The Pavilion also forms the core of Brighton's cultural quarter along with its most immediate neighbours, the Dome, the Corn Exchange, the Pavilion Theatre, the Theatre Royal, Brighton & Hove Museum and Art Gallery, the Jubilee Library, and Komedia in the neighbouring North Laine.

   The story of the Pavilion – a thirty-five-year saga of high ambition and all-consuming passion – is as bold and implausible as that of Brighton itself. It begins with the first visit of George, Prince of Wales, to the up-and-coming fashionable seaside resort in 1783. After his clandestine marriage to Maria Fitzherbert two years later, she took a house in Brighton and the town became their secret hideaway.

RIGHT **The west front of the Royal Pavilion from Pavilion Gardens**

BELOW LEFT AND RIGHT
Brighton Dome Concert Hall.
The Dome's renovated
Concert Hall is a unique fusion
of classic Regency styling and
1930s Art Deco.

RIGHT The east corridor,
Brighton Dome

LEFT The Theatre Royal, New Road. From its makeshift origins in a barn on Castle Square to its first permanent residence in North Street from 1774, the stage has indulged its love affair with Brighton. The Theatre Royal, the town's principal playhouse, opened on New Road in 1807 as the 'New Theatre', a three-storey stuccoed building fronted by a classically inspired Doric colonnade. After much refurbishment it reopened in 1866 as the Theatre Royal under new management, and was transformed by theatrical impresarios Nye and Nellie Chart into one of the country's leading provincial theatres. More alterations were undertaken in 1894, providing its present livery of red brick and terracotta, perched on paired Corinthian columns. Over the years, like an immaculately tailored matinee idol, it has charmed the loveliest of luvvies from Lauren Bacall and Marlene Dietrich to Peter O'Toole and Noel Coward.

The Prince in his turn leased a modest farmhouse overlooking the Old Steine and began almost immediately to plan its expansion. His London architect Henry Holland was commissioned to enlarge and refashion the humble 'Brighton House' into a Marine Pavilion, a residence more in keeping with his client's royal status. Holland replicated the farmhouse, connecting the two buildings by a rotunda with a shallow dome in the classical style.

While Holland was working on the Marine Pavilion, the Prince called on the services of architect William Porden to extend his Pavilion estate with a grand stable block (now Brighton Dome Concert Hall) and a riding school (the Corn Exchange). Influenced by the recently built Corn Exchange in Paris, and inspired by the watercolours of William and Thomas Daniell in *Views of Oriental Scenery*, Porden created an Indo-Saracenic dome that was monumental in scale, cost and ambition. At the time of its construction in 1804–1808, the giant dome, 24 metres (80 feet) in diameter and 20 metres (65 feet) in height, was one of the largest in the world, completely upstaging George's modest neoclassical bolt-hole. So bold was Porden's undertaking that it was widely feared that it might collapse once the scaffold was removed.

An underground passage was built in about 1822, running between the Dome and the northern end of the Pavilion. By this time, the Prince had become King George IV, and had long since abandoned Maria Fitzherbert for a series of mistresses. Rumours therefore have abounded of illicit royal trysts, but when the passage was constructed, George was so overweight and riddled with gout that his philandering days were more or less behind him.

The Dome was purchased by the town in 1850 as part of the Pavilion estate, and by 1867 had been appropriated as a magnificent assembly hall. Eighty years later it had reinvented itself once more as the town's principal concert hall. After a number of facelifts, including a multi-million pound millennial refurbishment and restoration, it is now, along with the Corn Exchange and adjacent Pavilion Theatre, one of the country's premier performing arts venues.

When the Dome was used as the royal stables, the fact that the Prince's horses were housed in greater luxury than himself attracted satirical scorn. In the face of public indignity, George did the only sensible thing: he set about transforming his Marine Pavilion into a magnificent Mughal fantasia – Kubla Khan's stately pleasure dome made manifest on the coast of England. There was one hurdle to overcome, however: funds. The interior of the Pavilion had been converted from classic French style into exotic Chinoiserie by Crace & Sons in 1802, while in 1806/7 Porden and Humphry Repton submitted plans for a new Indo-Chinese exterior, both of which were rejected due to lack of finance.

When George became Prince Regent in 1811, a change took place in his financial fortunes and he was finally able to set the wheels in motion to make his vision for the Brighton Pavilion a reality. Surveyor-General James Wyatt estimated the alterations at around £200,000, but died a year later and was replaced as chief architect by John Nash.

Nash extended and expanded upon Holland's original construction with exotic architectural flourishes in 'Hindoo' and Mahometan styles. He explored the very latest construction techniques, creating a cast-iron mantle over Holland's Pavilion to build domes, pagodas and minarets. These were then clothed in a delicate pierced stone screen, rendered and painted to create the impression of a unified building cast in Bath stone.

The development in all took seven years and was finally completed, or at least reached a sort of decorative impasse, in 1823, by which time the Prince Regent had succeeded to the throne. From the spectacular banqueting room to the state-of-the-art kitchen, the Royal Pavilion provided the ultimate in comfort and entertainment. Every luxury was afforded and no expense was spared in the pursuit of pleasure.

A veritable army of footmen and housemaids, physicians and apothecaries, masters of music, keepers of swans, removers of ashes and killers of rats was gainfully employed. Ice – when none was available locally – was imported from Norway to chill the hors d'oeuvres, and a private orchestra was maintained to entertain assembled guests.

The famous Chinoiserie interior had been created by the firm of Crace & Sons and the designer Robert Jones, but owes every inch of its opulent eccentricity to the man for whom it was built, the Prince of Wales. From the Banqueting Hall with its gilt dragon emerging from an azure-blue saucer ceiling to the 26,000 hand-gilded cockle-shells that make up the glittering firmament of the Music Room's vast dome, the Pavilion interior is a superlatively singular vision, a work of art designed with the express purpose of making you sit up and take notice. It was built during an age of ostentation, for a true fashionista. And whatever your reaction, it is hard to remain indifferent to its optical assault. Every decorative conceit – iron cast to resemble bamboo, imitation painted skylights, mirrored doors – every trick of light, scale and perspective – was contrived to create an effect upon the visitor that would build cumulatively until your senses were saturated with its technicolor splendour.

ABOVE LEFT Gloucester Road, North Laine

ABOVE RIGHT Housed in an old bus depot on North Road, Bill's café-cum-deli-cum-produce store is Brighton café culture at its most hip.

LEFT The Jubilee Library, shortlisted in 2005 for the Stirling Prize for architecture, is one of the most energy-efficient buildings in Britain. Designed by Bennetts Associates with Lomax Cassidy + Edwards, it is a fine example of twenty-first-century 'intelligent' architecture. Though it is constructed entirely from modern materials, its thousands of blue and green hand-glazed ceramic tiles echo the 'mathematical' patterning of many earlier Brighton buildings. Its vast interior takes its inspiration from the nineteenth-century Paris libraries of Henri Labrouste.

OPPOSITE ABOVE Bond Street, North Laine

OPPOSITE BELOW Bow-windowed cottages dating from the 1820s in Frederick Gardens, North Laine.

Ironically, just as the Royal Pavilion was finally completed the King's romance with Brighton had palled, and he was already making plans for his permanent retreat to London. In fact he only visited his new oriental palace three times between 1823 and 1827. When George IV died in 1830, he was succeeded by his brother William who changed the Pavilion's designation to the Royal Palace, Brighton, paying regular visits throughout his short reign. Their niece, Queen Victoria, however, was less enamoured, protesting that 'The people are very indiscreet and troublesome here . . . really; it makes this place quite a prison.' In 1850 George's pleasure palace was sold to the Corporation of Brighton for £50,000.

Throughout the following hundred years it assumed a number of guises – assembly rooms, art gallery and even military hospital during the First World War – before the long road to restoration began. Today it is a meticulously preserved reminder of Brighton's unique ancestry. It is also a fitting talisman to a city whose continued adherence to the creed of pleasure shows little sign of waning.

The North Laine

If the Royal Pavilion is the cornerstone of the city's cultural quarter, then the North Laine is the bustling heart of 'Bohemian' Brighton. Sandwiched between Trafalgar Street and North Street, its shop-lined avenues and intersecting paths began life as one of five large fields or 'laines' that lay north of the Old Town towards the open downland beyond.

'Laine' itself derives from an Anglo-Saxon term meaning lease or loan, a local Sussex word for open arable strips let to and farmed by tenant husbandmen. Each laine was divided and subdivided into parcels: 'furlongs' and smaller 'paul-pieces', separated by pathways or 'leakways', creating a mediaeval grid system of land cultivation that greatly influenced the shape of subsequent residential and commercial development.

As the eighteenth-century town prospered, North Street became its commercial hub, and everything north of this was soon developed for low-cost artisan housing and industry, precipitated by the coming of the railway. Despite Brighton's growing prosperity, however, and the development of foundries and sawmills to support the Volks Railway, Chain Pier and later the railway itself, when the manufacturing base began to decline the North Laine area eventually became one of the town's most deprived slum districts. A combination of over-crowding, poor sanitation and substandard housing gave rise to endemic disease and entrenched poverty. At its worst, in the notorious Pimlico and Orange Row quarters (the latter home to bricklayer turned bare-knuckle boxing champion Tom Sayers), open cesspits, slaughterhouses and the putrid air from confined living ultimately led to systematic slum clearance. By the mid-1960s the entire area was earmarked for destruction and redevelopment.

ABOVE Great Eastern
Public House, Trafalgar Street,
North Laine

RIGHT North Road,
North Laine

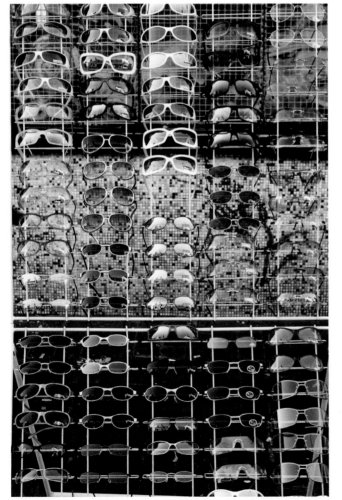

Against all odds and many instincts, the North Laine was designated a conservation area in 1977, and over the last quarter of a century has transformed itself from post-industrial inner-city black spot to one of the town's most vibrant quarters. Today its former barracks, foundries and warehouses, its dimly lit back streets, where Harry Cowley's barrow boys used to ply their bric-a-brac wares, have evolved into a scaled-down hybrid of New York's Greenwich Village and London's Camden Lock with aspirations to designer 'loft style' living. Decidedly hip and unashamedly kitsch, it has become the heartland of Brighton's alternative scene, an eclectic mix of retro chic and fetish culture, where café bars, junk stores and reclamation yards rub shoulders with tattoo parlours, wholefood delis and niche boutiques.

TOP LEFT **Komedia, Gardner Street, North Laine, is one of Brighton's top music, cabaret, theatre and comedy venues.**

BELOW FAR LEFT **Kensington Gardens, North Laine**

BELOW LEFT **North Laine**

BELOW **Sydney Street, North Laine**

the lanes/old quarter

'To see the Lanes at their best you should visit them at that magic hour when twilight is deepening into night. The shadows that have been lurking there for centuries slide from their corners and throw their dark hoods over the old houses. The queer old places seem to be falling asleep . . . they nod and lean forward their upper stories as if seeking the support of their neighbours while they drowse. Perhaps in the darkness they are whispering secrets . . . of the raids by the French, of the adventures of Charles, of the amours of Prince George.'

George Aitchison, *Unknown Brighton*, 1926

Brighton's latticework of lanes and twittens (a Sussex word used to describe a narrow path between two walls or hedges) criss-cross the historic heart of the city.

Today's Lanes are a designated conservation area, and an instant draw for hordes of visitors who trawl their jewellery stores and antique shops. Their charms, however, have not always been so apparent. Cramped and unkempt, these arthritic alleyways were for centuries home to sailors, smugglers, publicans, paupers, artisans, and a whole community of working fishermen, crammed together in cacophonous and no doubt malodorous proximity.

The Old Town developed as a consequence of mediaeval expansion. As the Lower Town outgrew its dwindling foreshore, its inhabitants began to populate and develop the flat open area flanked by West and East Streets and topped and tailed by North Street and the sea. The original fishermen's cottages were diminutive, squat dwellings of flint and chalk rubble, huddled together as if, by a collective effort of will, they could fend off the elements and the threat from across the Channel. However, the Old Town was virtually burned to the ground by the French in 1514, and though the concatenation of narrow alleyways and overhanging eaves still resonate with a ghostly

RIGHT The Friends' Meeting House on the corner of Prince Albert Street was constructed for Brighton's Quaker community in 1805. It should not be confused with Meeting House Lane, a small twitten said to be haunted by the ghost of a nun who was walled up alive after eloping with a soldier.

LEFT Antique and jewellery shopping in the Lanes

BELOW The Mock Turtle Tea Rooms, Pool Valley

mediaeval provenance, today's Old Quarter is predominantly a redevelopment of the eighteenth and nineteenth centuries.

Before the French raids changed forever the face of Tudor Brightelmstone, the Priory of St Bartholomew had stood at the heart of the quarter for some three hundred years. It was established as a monastic farm between 1120 and 1147 by the Cluniac Priory of Lewes on a site where Black Lion Street, Nile Street and Prince Albert Street now converge. What remained of the priory and chapel after the French sacking was dismantled in 1547 as a consequence of Henry VIII's sweeping Dissolution of the Monasteries. The land was first used to build almshouses, and from the 1730s to re-site Brighton's weekly market until the new Town Hall was constructed in 1830–32. Rumour has it that on discovering an ancient cemetery while excavating, the workforce could only be coaxed back to their task on the assurance that the monks had been Catholic. It is also conjectured that the wife-selling scene in *The Mayor of Casterbridge* was inspired by Thomas Hardy's visits to Brighton's marketplace, where the practice was, by all accounts, not uncommon.

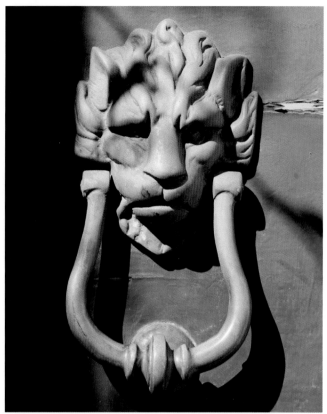

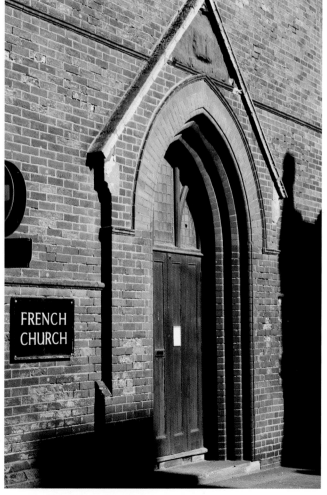

ABOVE English's Fish Restaurant and Oyster Bar. Occupying three former fishermen's cottages, the bow-fronted English's has been an oyster bar-cum-seafood restaurant of some renown for over 150 years, plying the likes of Laurence Olivier and Vivien Leigh with lobster bisque and Tattinger in velveteen Edwardian splendour. The Oyster Bar began life as Brazier's fishmongers. At the turn of the twentieth century a Brazier daughter married an English son and the rest, as they say, is history.

TOP RIGHT The Lanes

RIGHT The French Protestant Reformed Church, Queensbury Mews

66

LEFT The rather plain yellow brick façade of Middle Street Synagogue does little to suggest what lies beyond. But once inside, the interior reveals itself in a profusion of red marble, stained glass and gold mosaic. Built in 1874 by Thomas Lainson, surveyor of the Wick estate, it replaced an early nineteenth-century synagogue in Devonshire Place as the centre for Brighton's Jewish community. The original interior was unadorned, but patronage from the Sassoon family transformed it into one of the most richly decorative synagogues in all Europe.

RIGHT A Georgian doorcase, Middle Street

FAR RIGHT Ship Street

The Lanes themselves – centred on Union Street, Meeting House Lane and Brighton Square – were built on the old Hempshares, an area of flat ground set back from the sea where hemp was processed for rope to support the town's fishing industry. As the fortunes of the fishing fleets changed, smuggling of contraband supplemented depleted earnings, and the network of tunnels, built beneath the Old Town primarily for the transportation of coal, were put to more covert use.

As the Old Town grew in the late eighteenth and early nineteenth centuries, many of the fishermen's cottages were turned into shops and workrooms, initially for fishmongers and coal merchants, and then bootmakers, cabinet-makers, bakers, and as alehouses and boarding rooms. Cheap functional accommodation was constructed in and around the Lanes to service the fashionable new developments on the Steine, Castle Square and East Street. But as the town prospered and began to flaunt its new-found status, great acts of architectural expansion, including newer, smarter shops beyond the edges of the Old Town, left the Lanes outmoded and 'unworthy' of Brighton's modern aspirations.

ABOVE LEFT One of the last remnants of Hanningtons, which was a Brighton retail institution from 1805 to 2001.

BELOW LEFT A mosaic detail in the old Lanes

RIGHT Two seahorses adorn the facade of Brighton Hippodrome.

Decline set in and the area degenerated to such an extent that it was considered a serious candidate for wholesale slum clearance right up to the 1930s. Though much of the area met just such a fate, and many surviving antiquities were swallowed up in redevelopment, what remains has been preserved for posterity and stands as a poignant reminder of the city's modest beginnings.

Today, the Lanes are a thriving tourist hotspot and a collector's Mecca. Towards the end of the nineteenth century, as the grand houses of Britain's great spa towns were sold off and subdivided, antique-hunting and curio-collecting became highly profitable pursuits. As with the Pantiles in Tunbridge Wells, Brighton's Lanes were transformed into a cornucopia of Victoriana, *objets d'art*, and the bric-a-brac of centuries of accumulation.

Not surprisingly, the Lanes and twittens are conduits of local folklore, brimming with tales of hauntings and smugglers. Black Lion Lane, one of its narrowest twittens, can not only boast to have witnessed the unceremonious exit of King Charles II, borne along its length on the back of a fisherman, but also lay claim to one of the city's most regaled tales of Regency misadventure. The Barrymore brothers, a trio of profligate Irish aristocrats, were boon companions of George, Prince of Wales, charming him with their spontaneous acts of derring-do. They were known to their friends as Hellgate, Cripplegate and Newgate, while their sister was Billingsgate on account of her colourful turn of phrase. Most of their adventures involved wild and reckless wagers, in which no subject was considered too trivial or unseemly – from cat swallowing (fortunately the cat in question was never procured) – to riding a horse up Mrs Fitzherbert's staircase.

On one occasion a portly gentleman of the name Bullock wagered that he could outrun the young Lord Barrymore, given the choice of route and a head start. Cannily, Bullock chose

RIGHT The Gothic lantern and timber spire of St Paul's Church on West Street was restored in 1947 thanks to patronage by Haile Selassie, King of Kings, Lion of Judah and Emperor of Ethiopia, following a visit to Brighton during his exile after the Italian occupation of his homeland.

The quarter's oldest inn, the seventeenth-century Cricketers' Arms, was formerly called the Last and Fishcart, a 'last' being a measure of 10,000 herrings. The flint-faced Druid's Head is said to be haunted by the ghost of a man bricked up in a tunnel beneath the cellars. The Market Inn, née the Three Chimneys, was once owned by the Prince of Wales' chimney sweep. The Sussex Tavern (1816) stands on the site of a renowned haunt for seventeenth-century smugglers. The Pump House (1776) is named after the town well that once stood nearby on the Knab. The Bath Arms (1864) was converted from two shops – a greengrocers and milliners – and concealed beneath it is the sealed-up entrance to a network of tunnels that traverse the old lanes in a dark subterranean nexus.

Of all these, the Black Lion Pub (in itself a fairly recent reconstruction of the old Black Lion Brewery) has perhaps the most colourful story. Legend has it that the original brewery, named after the Black Lion of Flanders, was established in 1546 by Flemish immigrant Deryk Carver, who grew hops on the Hempshare. It is more likely, however, that he owned an inn of the same name on the other side of the street.

Carver was the first Protestant to be martyred during the reign of Mary Tudor. Found guilty of heresy for reading the Bible in English, he was burned in a barrel outside the Star Inn in Lewes High Street on 22 July 1555. As a final gesture of defiance he is said to have hurled his Bible into the crowd. Some hundred or so years later, family descendant Thomas Carver was also touched by immortality. As the mate of the ship *Surprise*, it was he who ferried King Charles II on his back through the surf to make his escape to France. In return for his service, the young Carver requested the release of imprisoned Quakers and nonconformists, famously rebuking the King's original offer of six detainees as 'a poor exchange for a king's ransom'. Among those finally set free was John Bunyan, author of *The Pilgrim's Progress*.

Black Lion Lane and, due to his considerable girth, prevented Barrymore from passing, as he ambled to victory much to the amusement of the young Prince and his fellow speculators. Not renowned for their restraint, the Barrymores' favourite night-time distraction, when not swapping street signs around, was to prop an open coffin, complete with a servant made over as corpse, against the door of an unsuspecting household, knock and then run for cover.

If the Lanes have secrets to reveal, then the pubs and old coaching inns at every corner of the Old Town are repositories of fact, fiction and whatever lies between. Each tells its own tale, offering a useful perspective on the evolution of the area.

LEFT English's Seafood
Restaurant

BELOW Stained glass
impression of the West Pier
from the Heist Bar on
West Street.

hove

Hove, Brighton's immediate neighbour and historical sparring partner, has defended itself throughout its history against its rival's attempts at annexation. The much parodied but still widely bandied epithet 'Hove Actually' has been the symbol of its defiant will to retain separateness. Despite the fact that Hove was part of the parliamentary constituency of Brighton from the Great Reform Act of 1832 until 1949, and that the two boroughs were finally merged in 1997 and transformed into the new millennium city by the sea in 2000, there remains little consensus of identity.

Modern Hove incorporates within its administrative boundaries the outlying environs of Hangleton, Aldrington, West Blatchington and Portslade, but for brevity's sake this whistle-stop historical tour concentrates on its central extent from the old village boundary in the west to the Brunswick estate on the borders of Brighton.

While Brighton found its feet in an age of decadence and liberal excess, and had thereafter a somewhat raffish reputation, its younger sibling was the product of a less forgiving epoch. Though the ancient parish of Hove in fact dates back some eight centuries, what remains today is essentially a Victorian invention, formed in the shadow of its cosmopolitan neighbour as a genteel and rather more 'conservative' resort town favoured by the discerning middle classes.

Like Brighton, the mediaeval fishing village of Hove grew up on a dwindling foreshore, subject to continual erosion and the vicissitudes of the elements. But, whereas Brighton developed into a thriving fishing community, Hove remained a sparsely populated and comparatively impoverished agricultural settlement right up to the mid-nineteenth century. In 1801 its population was just 101, and by the 1820s, at the height of Brighton's Regency glory, it still comprised little more than the ancient parish church of St Andrew's surrounded by farmsteads and open fields. Its single street, Hove Drove (now

RIGHT **Brunswick Square**

100

Hove Street), ran down to a huddle of fishermen's cottages and curing-houses on the seafront.

The first indication of a change in Hove's fortunes was the transformation of the chalybeate spring at St Anne's Well. However, the single greatest catalyst for the suburbanisation of the small parish was the creation of the Brunswick and Adelaide estates to its east. Brunswick was conceived as a western equivalent of the Kemp Town estate, an elegant seafront terrace backed by a grand square and serviced by stable yards, public baths, a large covered market, hostelries and service streets for coachmen and tradesmen. Today the area contains numerous listed buildings and is regarded as one of the finest examples of Regency and early Victorian civic planning anywhere in the country.

Though the architectural partnership of Wilds and Busby once again received the commission, the enterprise was in fact more or less a solo undertaking, bearing all the hallmarks of Charles Busby's distinctive design aesthetic: a harmonious and unifying vision of man and nature brought to life in a glorious neo-classical style. Its Corinthian columns, pilasters and vertical fenestration were influenced in part by the young architect's sojourn in Washington DC, particularly the classical façade of the Capitol building.

Work commenced in 1824, approximately a year after Kemp Town, on part of the Wick estate owned by the Rev. Thomas Scutt, and by 1830 both Brunswick Terrace and Brunswick Square were complete. Unlike Kemp Town, the estate was an immediate success, the houses either bought by speculators and builders and sold on for a quick profit or rented out as fully furnished retreats for the winter season.

In the same year an Act of Parliament, one of the last under George IV, decreed that the estate be managed by the newly

ABOVE LEFT **Brunswick Square.** As part of the 1830 Brunswick Square Act, a covenant was drawn up dictating that all purchasers must stucco the outside of their houses with Parker's cement and paint every three years, a stipulation that is still in force today (though now extended to every five years).

ABOVE RIGHT **Vernacular architecture, Brunswick Town**

LEFT AND BELOW Regency Townhouse, Brunswick Square. Between the wars Brunswick, by now predominantly flats and bedsits, fell into such disrepair that Hove Council seriously considered its demolition. This proposal thankfully met with stiff opposition and spawned the formation of the Regency Society, a conservation body dedicated to preserving Brighton and Hove's Regency heritage. The Regency Townhouse, at No. 13 Brunswick Square, is a Grade I listed terraced house of the mid-1820s being developed as a heritage centre and museum to focus on the architecture and social history of Brighton and Hove between the 1780s and the 1840s.

LEFT, RIGHT AND AND BELOW
The Brunswick estate church
of St Andrew's in Waterloo
Street was not conceived
as part of Busby's original
design. Instead it was
commissioned by the Rev.
Edward Everard and built in
1828 by Charles Barry. The
architecture is revolutionary in
that Barry drew his inspiration
from the Italian Renaissance
rather than from Antiquity.
St Andrew's soon became the
most fashionable church in
Brighton. So that the different
classes of worshipper would
not have to cross paths after
the service, there were three
separate entrance doors. A
discreet tunnel, which ran from
the church to the Kerrison
Arms Hotel opposite, provided
an exclusive escape route
for the assembled aristocracy.
St Andrew's is currently in
the care of the Churches
Conservation Trust.

FAR LEFT Boundary Passage marks the border between Brighton and Hove.

LEFT Osborne Villas, Cliftonville

BELOW Church Road

RIGHT Hove's coat of arms

FAR RIGHT The Avenues. Many of Brighton's Georgian and Regency developments were built as grand-fronted stuccoed façades, behind which all manner of ills were concealed in the form of 'bungaroosh', a shoddy amalgam of flint, chalk and rubble. The houses of Cliftonville and the Avenues mark a transition from bungaroosh to brick.

formed Brunswick Commissioners, forerunners of the Hove Commissioners, 1875, and the Hove Corporation, 1898, lending the estate far greater autonomy than even Thomas Kemp ever dreamed of and effectively constituting a self-sufficient municipal district. Eventually Brunswick incorporated its own fire services, police station, magistrate's court and town hall.

Though its residents never quite matched Kemp Town for prestige and royal patronage, in its heyday Brunswick attracted an impressive line-up of British and European aristocrats, ministers and foreign diplomats who took its townhouses and terraces on short-term lets for the fashionable season from September to February. These included Sir Robert Peel, William Ewart Gladstone, Lord Chancellor Brougham, the Marquis of Wellesley (the Duke of Wellington's brother), the Duke and Duchess of Gloucester, Princess Lieven and the Austrian Chancellor, Prince Metternich.

As for Busby, like Thomas Kemp before him, he was caught in the throes of feverish property speculation, and over-extended himself on the cusp of an economic slump. At the time of his death in 1834 he was virtually bankrupt, leaving a meagre estate of £200. His architectural legacy, however, lived on well into the Victorian era, influencing the sweeping lines

of Decimus Burton's Adelaide Crescent, which continued the Regency march westwards towards Hove.

Work on Adelaide Crescent began in 1830 on the remainder of the Wick estate for its new owner, philanthropist and financier Sir Isaac Goldsmid. Palmeira Square, named in Goldsmid's honour (he had been created Baron da Goldsmid e da Palmeira in the Portuguese peerage), was constructed on the site of one of history's lesser-known architectural misadventures: an enormous cast-iron and glass conservatory known as the Anthaeum. Designed by A.H. Wilds, and constructed from 40,000 square feet (3,700 square metres) of glass, the 160-foot (48-metre) wide arboretum-cum-pleasure-garden was the largest dome of its kind in the world; bigger than St Peter's in Rome. Its glory, however, was cruelly cut short. Wilds and the chief engineer had already resigned because of their concerns about safety shortcuts, and on the eve of its opening, on 31 August 1833, the entire building collapsed. The debris lay scattered across the site for some twenty years before work on Palmeira began in earnest in 1855.

Though they were technically built in the parish of Hove, both the Brunswick and Adelaide estates were considered to be very much part of Brighton, signifying the town's western

extent, beyond which still lay open fields and beyond that the village of Hove itself.

Legislation at the time prohibited building immediately west of Brunswick Town, on the Stanford estate, so the next suburban surge towards Hove proper was the mid-Victorian 'frontier town' of Cliftonville (Albany, Medina, Osborne and Ventnor Villas), built some 20 acres (9 hectares) east of the old village. In contrast to the classical unity of Brunswick, Cliftonville

evolved over a number of years, plot by plot, with no overall blueprint. The result is a gloriously eclectic mis-match of architectural styles and ambitions, including a nostalgic nod to the Regency.

The opening of the Cliftonville railway station in 1865 (later to become West Brighton station in 1879 and eventually Hove station in 1895) encouraged further development. In marked contrast to Brighton's Regency stucco, Cliftonville's terraces of large, bay-fronted, yellow-brick Victorian villas gave way to humbler workers' accommodation north of Church Road.

The development of Cliftonville had essentially 'leapfrogged' a wide tract of open land that remained fallow until the Stanford estate was finally opened up in 1871 to create 'West Brighton estate' or The Avenues. Like a mini-Manhattan in Italianate yellow-brick and Victorian domestic red-brick revival, the estate was a rectangular grid of wide numbered avenues – First, Second, Third, Fourth and Grand – that plugged the only remaining gap in the linear sprawl that now ran uninterrupted from Kemp Town to Hove Village.

LEFT ABOVE AND BELOW
Lansdowne Place

RIGHT **Palmeira Square**

While Brighton can boast enough celebrity fodder to satisfy even the most demanding of appetites, Hove can, if pressed, summon up a perfectly respectable roll-call of its own. Sir Winston Churchill was schooled here, as was Patrick Hamilton, author of *Rope*, *Gaslight* and his masterpiece, *Hangover Square*. English Post-impressionist Robert Bevan was born here. Admiral Sir George Augustus Westphal, wounded in action aboard Nelson's flagship *Victory* at the Battle of Trafalgar, is buried here. As is Sir George Everest, Surveyor-General of India, after whom the world's tallest mountain was named in 1852.

It is not without a certain twist of irony that the somewhat dour younger sibling of one of Europe's undisputed glamour queens, should also at the turn of the twentieth century become a credible forerunner of Hollywood. From the 1880s many of the world's first true film pioneers – James Williamson, George Albert Smith, William Friese-Greene, Arthur Albert Esmé Collings – transformed Hove into a centre for film and cinema development. Some of the earliest studios were built within the parish, including George Albert Smith's studio, considered to be the first of its type in the world, in St Anne's Well

Gardens, and for a number of years Hove helped to kickstart a worldwide revolution in cinematography.

Hove's role in the birth of the moving-picture industry was short-lived. By the early twentieth century the London suburban studios at Elstree had taken over the lion's share of the United Kingdom's film production. Nevertheless, Hove's influence was significant, and with Brighton it became the

ABOVE **Gwydyr Saloon** in Palmeira Square, established as a barber's shop in 1890.

LEFT **Moulds for chocolates at Audrey's** in Holland Road. Audrey's have been producing hand-made chocolates on their premises in Hove since 1948. They make in the region of 15 tonnes of chocolates each year and supply, among other prestigious clients, Fortnum & Mason.

RIGHT **Little Preston Street**

BELOW RIGHT **Freemasons Restaurant**, Western Road

111

LEFT **The Drive, the Avenues**

ABOVE RIGHT **Albert Mews**

BELOW RIGHT Original beam
engine from No. 2 Engine
House, Goldstone Pumping
Station, now the British
Engineerium Museum of
mechanical antiquities.

FAR RIGHT **The Drive,
the Avenues**

location for numerous productions – from *The Gay Divorce* (1934) with Fred Astaire and Ginger Rogers to *The End of the Affair* (1999) with Ralph Fiennes and Julianne Moore, taking in *Brighton Rock* (1947), *Oh! What a Lovely War* (1969), and *Quadrophenia* (1979) along the way.

Hove may have missed a trick in not perpetuating its role as little Hollywood by the Sea, but over the years it has shaken off its rather staid image and begun to embrace the pleasure principle espoused for so long by its Georgian neighbour. From Hove Street in the west to Brunswick in the east, Hove has begun to indulge itself in café culture and flirt with twenty-first-century boutique couture.

As I write, plans for a controversial £250 million redevelopment of the King Alfred Centre on Hove seafront by architectural iconoclast Frank Gehry, with the aid of Anthony Gormley, Piers Gough and Brad Pitt, promise to be the boldest architectural statement the city has seen since A.H. Wilds' ill-fated Anthaeum. It has already stirred up a hornet's nest of opinion and speculation: for those who welcome its daring vision of a brave new Hove, and embrace its flamboyant symbolism, it represents an opportunity for Hove finally to relegate its quiet Victorian conservatism to the history books; for its opponents it is yet another affront to its proud gentility.

hanover &
queen's park

Hanover

Home to some of the city's finest public houses, narrowest streets and steepest hills, Hanover is a cosy residential neighbourhood. The tightly packed cream and pastel terraces are bordered to the west by Lewes Road, east by Queen's Park, north by Elm Grove and south by Albion Hill. In direct contrast to the middle-class developments of Montpelier and Clifton Hill, perched on the opposite crest across the valley of central Brighton, Hanover's comparatively humble terraces were built to accommodate the Victorian working classes, many of whom had relocated from less salubrious slum areas across the city. Today, in contrast, it is primarily a middle-class suburb of owner-occupiers. It is one of the few areas of the city where houses, due to their comparatively modest size, have not been subdivided into flats.

Though it dates back to the late eighteenth century – the Percy Almshouses at the bottom of Elm Grove were built in 1795 to house six poor widows – the main thrust of Hanover's development took off in the 1860s. Before this it was primarily open downland and arable fields or 'laines', interspersed with tenanted market gardens and bisected by footpaths and bridleways out to Rottingdean and beyond to Lewes. The farthest north any substantial development had spread was on the slopes of Carlton Hill, a conglomeration of tenements, public houses, slaughterhouses and artisan workshops that would become one of the town's most notorious slum blackspots.

Despite the area's distinctly working-class origins, one of Hanover's first developments (after the construction of the almshouses) was a crescent of grand neo-classical houses, built by A.H. Wilds in 1822, replete with bow fronts and

RIGHT Lincoln Street, Hanover

ABOVE LEFT **Built in 1795 for six poor widows, the Percy Almshouses were the first Gothic Revival buildings in Brighton.**

RIGHT **Ewart Street**

BELOW LEFT Archer's master butchers has been in Hanover for three generations and is one of the few survivors from a time when the area was a thriving community of family-run shops and small businesses. Archer's went organic back in 1987 and is something of a Brighton institution.

trademark ammonite pilasters. Hanover Crescent was one of a number of grand developments that had sprung up along the main Lewes Road, overlooking the recently laid out Level recreational fields and the Royal Gardens.

The latter, designed at roughly the same time as Hanover Crescent, was the site of the first county cricket ground in England (previously the Prince of Wales' own cricket pitch). Laid out by Regency entrepreneur James Ireland as a financial speculation, the pleasure gardens included, at the height of their fame, assembly rooms, an elevated promenade, an aviary, a grotto, a maze, and even a small menagerie. Due to lack of subscription and general neglect, however, the site soon fell into disrepair. It was redeveloped from 1849 by the ubiquitous Wilds as Park Crescent, an elegant horseshoe façade of high-class townhouses enclosing a large secluded private garden.

Slowly the land behind Hanover Crescent, the 'paul-pieces' and 'furlongs' of Hilly Laine, were developed, though the quality and size of housing was far more humble. Many of the residents were unskilled labourers or farm workers, often living two or three families to one squat terraced house. The open land between the half-built terraces and market gardens was used as drying fields for hand laundries, a home-grown industry that at one point employed forty-two laundresses in Hanover Terrace alone.

As tradesmen – carpenters, gardeners, grooms, stable hands and later locomotive workers – began to flock to the area, a sizeable community grew up, supported by a surge of local amenities: small shops, mission houses, public houses, public baths, poor houses and chapels, many of which doubled up as schools.

At the centre of the community was the Church of the Annunciation, built in 1864 for philanthropist and champion of Brighton's disenfranchised poor, Father Arthur Douglas Wagner, who, against the grain of common practice, dispensed with the prevalent system of pew rental in order to accommodate the predominantly working-class congregation. The church was substantially rebuilt over the years and in 1892 a tower and short spire were added, complete with stained glass by Edward Burne-Jones and William Morris. The church was also to become one of the cornerstones of the high church Anglo-Catholic 'ritualist' debate of the day.

ABOVE LEFT **Hanover Street**

ABOVE RIGHT **Park Crescent's horseshoe façade was constructed by A.H. Wilds from 1849 around the former Royal Gardens cricket ground.**

One of the more notable members of the church's congregation was *fin de siècle* illustrator and renowned decadent Aubrey Beardsley, who was greatly influenced by the ritualistic elements of its Anglo-Catholic ceremonies. Beardsley, who had achieved notoriety by illustrating Oscar Wilde's *Salome* and the *Yellow Book*, eventually converted to the Roman Catholic Church before his premature death from tuberculosis at the age of twenty-five.

If Hanover's spiritual needs were served well by Wagner's philanthropy and the houses of worship that became his legacy, then its more immediate material wants were met by another man of vision, whose public houses attracted an equally zealous form of devotion. Richard Tamplin's Phoenix Brewery, established in the town from 1821 after rising from the ashes of a fire in Southwick, had expanded to such an extent by 1902 that it had become the largest in the country, occupying over 100,000 square feet (9,300 square metres) from the bottom of Albion Street to Southover Street. It employed over 150 men and eventually extended its reach to include two hundred of Brighton's licensed premises and over four hundred beyond its

fringes. In 1800 Brighton could boast one pub per thirty houses (compared with one for every six thousand in 1998). In Hanover alone there was, and in many cases still is, a public house or inn on every street corner. By 1879 there were eight inns on Southover Street alone.

Today, Hanover's churches and ale-houses are essentially all that remain of its working-class roots. And though it retains a proud sense of community, which spills over each year with convivial *joie de vivre* on to the streets for the annual Hanover Day celebrations, beer festival and Artists' Trail, the local businesses that used to throng its steep streets have almost all disappeared, along with its schools, garages and dairies. Gone are the days that Southover Street alone could boast three barbers, three butchers, three newsagents, three boot repairers, one laundry, four greengrocers, two chemists and seven grocers. Modern Hanover is as upwardly mobile as the rest of twenty-first-century Brighton, though its multi-coloured terraces and profusion of watering holes conceal, beneath the veneer of Ikea, a side of Brighton's history that is all too often lost in the footnotes of its grand Regency narrative.

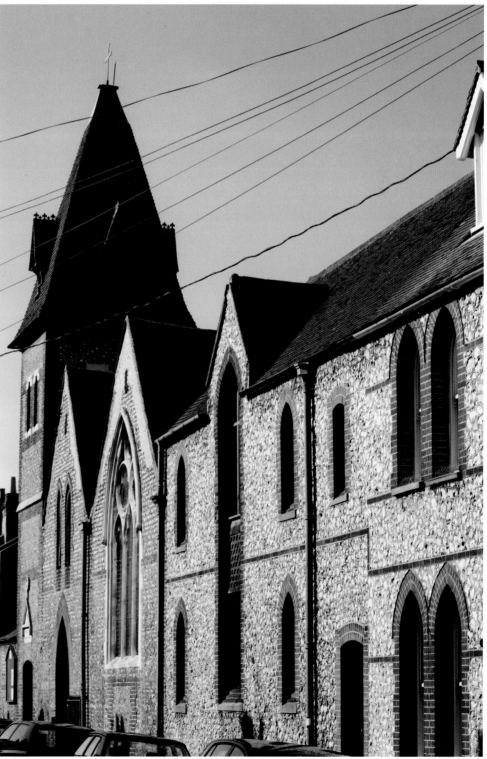

LEFT AND BELOW The former Tamplin & Sons Phoenix Brewery on Albion Street rose from the ashes of a fire in Southwick in 1820 to become by the turn of the century the largest brewery in England.

RIGHT Hanover Crescent

Queen's Park

At the height of her fame as a retreat for curative seawater bathing, Brighton had become renowned as the 'Queen of the watering holes'. However, she lacked one essential ingredient: a natural spa, without which she could hardly claim to rival the great English health resorts of Bath, Cheltenham and Tunbridge Wells.

The natural chalybeate spring at St Anne's Well had been developed by Dr Russell as a small spa from 1750, but it lay some distance from the town's fashionable centre and was not fully exploited until the 1830s. Never one to let practical considerations get in the way of aspiration, Dr F.A. Struve stepped up to the mark and simply invented one. A research chemist from Saxony, Dr Struve had already undertaken similar constructions at Leipzig and Berlin, and now 'created' an 'artificial' spa on the south-western corner of what today is Queen's Park.

Water from an artesian well was extracted and chemically refined with imported minerals to reproduce the healing properties of the natural waters of Pyrmont, Karlsbad (Karlovy Vary) and the other great European resorts. The spa itself was housed in an ornate neo-classical pump room complete with

Ionic portico and grand saloon. It was an immediate success, drawing the great and good of Regency Society, who subscribed in their hundreds. Soon it gained the royal seal of approval, and was renamed the 'Royal German Spa' in honour of William IV, one of its more prestigious patrons. At the peak of its success – the mid-1830s – a cavalcade of carriages snaked its way from the park entrance to the sea.

Its fame, however, was short-lived, and by the mid-1850s it had fallen out of fashion. Struve – by now answering to the title of Knight of the Saxon Order of Civil Merit and Fidelity – turned his hand instead to the production of bottled mineral water, the manufacture of which continued from the spa right up until 1963. The building eventually fell into decline and the pump room was demolished, though its neo-classical façade was restored in the late 1970s as the site for a nursery school.

When Thomas Attree – solicitor by appointment to the royal family and rival to Thomas Kemp as Brighton's most eminent citizen – purchased Brighton Park in 1829, it consisted of a 15-acre private garden that had been laid out five years earlier for a Mr John Armstrong, with access available by subscription only. Inspired by Regent's Park in London, Attree immediately commissioned Charles Barry to build a grand Italianate villa,

part of a planned estate of large mansion houses fringing his own private park. In the event, only his own villa was built. Barry had already designed Brighton's St Peter's Church (1824–8), one of the earliest Gothic Revival churches in the country, and was later to become the celebrated architect of the Houses of Parliament. Attree's plans also included two impressive entrance gates at Egremont Place and Park Street and the distinctive 'Pepper Pot', a ten-sided, 20-metre (60-foot) high tower, presumably built to house the villa's pump and water tank. Attree renamed the gardens Queen's Park in 1836 in honour of Queen Adelaide, wife of William IV, and introduced, among other innovations, an aviary and an archery range.

Attree, who was something of a philanthropist, according to one popular story, bequeathed a crown piece ('Attree Gold') to every septuagenarian Brighton citizen. Despite his altruistic bent, the park was a private enclosure for invited guests only, and remained the sole province of the 'socially connected' right up until his death in 1863 at the ripe old age of eighty-five.

This situation continued for another three decades. After Attree's death the villa and park were bought by Hong Kong publishing entrepreneur and property tycoon George Duddell

who, among other extravagances, had an extensive roller-skating rink constructed as the centrepiece of his own exclusive gardens. Following his death, the villa was appropriated as a Catholic college for boys, before falling into disrepair in the late 1960s. Despite its Grade II listing as a building of outstanding historical interest, it was finally demolished in 1972.

Today all that remains of Attree's original vision is the villa's mini garden gazebo and the 'Pepper-pot' tower, which over the years has been requisitioned as a printing press for the *Brighton Daily Mail*, as an observation tower during the Second World War, as a Scout hut, and an artist's studio.

The park itself was acquired on behalf of the town by the Race Stand Trustees in 1891, and re-landscaped before its grand opening in August 1892 as an ornamental public garden complete with a large lake excavated on the site of Duddell's roller-skating rink. Though it was once arguably Brighton's grandest ornamental park, perched high above the urban sprawl and fronted by large red-brick, High Victorian and early Edwardian townhouses, its elegance is somewhat faded. Today it takes quite a leap of imagination to summon its former glory.

124

ABOVE LEFT **Former Municipal Technical College**

ABOVE RIGHT **Brighton's Technical College began life as the Brighton School of Art and Science in the great kitchen of the Royal Pavilion in 1858. This Renaissance style red-brick building on Richmond Terrace was formally opened as the Municipal Technical College in 1898. It has recently been converted into flats.**

RIGHT The original entrance
arches to Queen's Park were
rebuilt in 1890, inscribed with
the names of the Race Stand
Trustees who presented the
park to the town in 1892.

BELOW LEFT The Pepper Pot,
Queen's Park, was the former
water tower of Thomas
Attree's villa.

BELOW RIGHT St Peter's
Church

RIGHT St Peter's Church was built between 1824 and 1828 as a chapel of ease to the parish church of St Nicholas. Much to the dismay of Brighton's resident architectural partnership, Wilds and Busby, Charles Barry was granted the commission, as the result of a competition to select a new design. It is one of the earliest Gothic Revival churches in England.

bibliography

Aitchison, George, *Unknown Brighton*, The Bodley Head Ltd, London, 1926

Beckett, R.B. (ed.), *John Constable's Correspondence: VI: The Fishes*, Ipswich, 1968

Beevers, David (ed.), *Brighton Revealed through Artists' Eyes c.1760–1960*, Royal Pavilion, Art Gallery and Museums, Brighton, 1995

Bingham, Neil, *C.A. Busby, The Regency Architect of Brighton & Hove*, RIBA Heinz Gallery, 1991

Bramwell, David, *The Cheeky Guide to Brighton*, Cheekyguides Ltd, Brighton, 2004

Carder, Timothy, *The Encyclopaedia of Brighton*, East Sussex County Libraries, Brighton, 1990

Catching Stories: Voices from the Brighton Fishing Community, QueenSpark Books, Brighton, 1996

Dale, Anthony, *Fashionable Brighton 1820–1860*, Country Life Ltd, London,1947

Fiennes, K., *A History of Brighton & Hove*, Phillimore & Co Ltd, Chichester, 2002

Flower, Raymond, *The Old Ship*, Croom Helm Ltd, London, 1986

Gilbert, Edmund W., *Brighton: Old Ocean's Bauble*, Methuen & Co Ltd, London, 1954

A Guide to the Buildings of Brighton, School of Architecture and Design, Brighton Polytechnic, Mcmillan Martin, Macclesfield, RIBA South East

Jones, Lavender & Pollard, Jacqueline, *Hilly Laine to Hanover: a Brighton Neighbourhood*, Brighton Books, Brighton,1999

Middleton, Judy, *A History of Hove*, Phillimore & Co Ltd, Chichester, 1979

Robinson, Leslie John, *The Lanes of Brighton*, Brighton, 1966

Rutherford, Jessica, *The Royal Pavilion: The Palace of George IV*, Royal Pavilion, Libraries & Museums, Brighton & Hove City Council, 1994

Seldon, Anthony, *Brave New City: Brighton & Hove, Past Present, Future*, Pomegranate Press, Lewes, 2002

Sitwell, Osbert & Barton, Margaret, *Brighton*, Faber & Faber, London, 1935

Wigan, Arthur Ladbroke, *Brighton and its Three Climates*, London, 1843

index

Adelaide Crescent, 107
Ainsworth, William Harrison, 57
Albany Villas, 107
Albert Mews, 113
Albion Street, 119
Anthaeum, 46, 107, 113
Archer's butchers, 117
Arundel Terrace, 44
Attree, Thomas, 123
Audrey's Chocolates, 110
Austen, Jane, 8
The Avenues, 106, 108, 112
Barry, Charles, 69, 104, 123, 124, 126
Barrymore brothers, 94
Beardsley, Aubrey, 21, 119
Beau Brummel, 16
Belgrave Place, 54
Bennett, Arnold, 21
Benson, E.F., 69
Bevan, Robert, 110
Birch, Eugenius, 19, 36
Black Lion Lane, 94
Black Lion Street, 36, 88
Black Rock, 38, 39, 44
Blaker Street, 17
Bodley, G.F., 71
Bond Street, 80
Borough Street, 67
Boundary Passage, 106
Brighton Centre, 23
Brighton College, 56
Brighton Festival, 17
Brighton & Hove High School for Girls, 61
Brighton Marina, 28, 29, 38, 39
Brighton Pier, 29, 30, 33, 35, 36, 37, 38, 39
Brougham, Lord Chancellor, 106
Brunswick, estate 7, 52, 100, 102–104; Prince Caroline of, 17; Square, 100, 102, 103, Terrace, 102
Bunyan, John, 96
Burges, William, 71
Burne-Jones, Edward, 21, 71, 118
Burton, Decimus, 107
Busby, Charles Augustin, 16, 46, 56, 61, 102, 104, 106, 126
Lord Byron, 17
Camelford Street, 51
Carden, Herbert, 22
Carew, John Edward, 57
Carlton Hill, 114
Carpenter, Richard Cromwell, 69
Carroll, Lewis, 54, 57
Carver, Deryk, 96; Thomas, 96
Castle Inn, 20
Cavendish, William, 6th Duke of Devonshire, 53

Cemetery; Extra-Mural, 12, 15; Jewish, 12
Chain Pier, 36, 82
Charles II, 12, 71, 94, 96
Churchill, Winston, 110
Church of the Annunciation, 118, 121
Church Road, 106, 108
Clifton, Hill, 7, 58, 67, 69, 114; Place, 63; Terrace, 61, 62, 69; Windmill, 61
Cliftonville, 106–108
Coates, Wells, 42
Cobbett, William, 72
Collings, Arthur Albert Esmé, 110
Constable, John, 17, 35
Conyngham, Lady, 17
Corn Exchange, 72, 79
Coward Noel, 21, 78
Crace & sons, 79, 80
Cubitt, Thomas, 46, 53
Cumberland, Duke of, 14, 53
Dale, Anthony, 17, 57
Dance, George, 67
Defoe, Daniel, 12, 32
Dome Concert Hall, 25, 72, 76
Duke of York's cinema, 10
Dickens, Charles, 8, 19, 20, 69
Duddell, George, 124
Dyke Road, 58
Edward VII, 21, 53
Egremont Place, 124
Elm Grove, 114
Eliot, T.S., 8
Embassy Court, 39, 42
Engineerium Museum, 112
English's Fish Restaurant, 89, 99
Everard, Rev. Edward 104
Everest, Sir George, 110
Ewart Street, 117
Fife, Duke and Duchess of, 53
Fishing Museum, 28, 29
Fitzherbert, Maria, 14, 17, 57, 72, 79, 94
Frederick Gardens, 80
Friese-Greene, William, 110
Friends Meeting House, 87
Fry, Roger, 21
Gehry, Frank, 113
George III, 14, 16
George IV, 16, 20, 79, 80, 102
George, Prince of Wales, 14, 17, 23, 34, 67, 72, 94
Gill, Eric, 24
Gladstone, William Ewart, 106
Gloucester, Duke and Duchess of, 106
Gloucester Road, 80
Goldsmid, Sir Isaac, 107
Gore, Spencer, 35
Grand Hotel, 38, 43
Greene, Graham, 21, 36, 67

Guildford Street, 65
Gunn, Martha, 15, 34, 71
Gwydyr Saloon, 110
Hamilton, Patrick, 110
Hampton Place, 69
Hanbury Ballroom, 50
Hannington's, 92
Hanover, 114–126; Crescent, 46, 67, 114, 118, 123; Street, 118, 120; Terrace, 118
Harding, Gilbert, 58
Hardy, Thomas, 88
Hazlitt, William, 72
Hempshares, 32, 91
Hessel, Phoebe, 15, 71
Hilly Laine, 118
Hippodrome, 93–95
Holland, Henry, 79, 80
Hove, 36, 58, 101–113
Hove Street, 102
Ireland, James, 118
Johnson, Samuel, 71
Jones, Robert, 80
Jubilee Library, 25, 72, 80
Kemp, Thomas Read, 16, 44-45, 53, 60, 71, 106
Kemp Town, 7, 36, 44-57, 106
Kempe, Charles Eamer, 71
Kendall, William, 52
Kensington Gardens, 84
King Alfred Centre, 113
King's Road, 36, 38, 39
Kipling, Rudyard, 21
Komedia, 72, 84
Lainson, Thomas, 90
Lansdowne Place, 109
The Lanes, 86-99
Lewes Crescent, 28, 44, 46, 47, 52, 53, 57
Lewes Road, 114, 118
Lieven, Princess, 104
Lincoln Street, 115
Little Preston Street, 110
London Road viaduct, 21
Lutyens, Sir Edwin, 57
Madeira Drive, 40
Madeira Lift, 46, 52
Madeira Terrace, 52
Maddox Brown, Ford, 71
Mahomed, Sake Dene, 71
Mantell, Gideon, 67
Marine Parade, 52, 53, 54
Marine Pavilion, 16, 79
Marine Square, 52
Medina Villas, 107
Meeting House Lane, 86, 91
Melville, Alan, 69
Metropole Hotel, 38
Metternich, Prince, Austrian Chancellor, 53
Middle Street, 90; Synagogue, 90
Miles, John 'Smoaker', 34

Montpelier, 58–71, 114; Crescent, 61, 67; Hall, 61; Place, 20,64; Road, 61, 67, 69; Terrace, 58, 61; Villas, 58, 59, 61
Morris, William, 71, 118
Morrissey, Charlie, 17
Museum and Art Gallery, 25, 72, 79
Nash, John, 46, 79–80
New Steine, 48
Nile Street, 88
North Laine, 72, 82-85
North Road, 83
North Street, 82
Novello, Ivor, 21
Olivier, Sir Laurence, 89, 94
Old Ship Hotel, 19, 20, 38
Oriental Place, 67
Orange Row, 82
Osborne Villas, 106
Otto, J.B., 46
Paganini, Nicolo, 17, 20
Palmeira Square, 107, 109, 110
Park Crescent, 118, 119
Park Street, 124
Pasquin, Anthony, 35
Pavilion Theatre, 72, 79
Peel, Sir Robert, 106
Pepper-pot, 124, 125
Percy Almshouses, 114, 116
Phillips, Henry, 46
Pool Valley, 26
Porden, William, 79
Port Hall, 11, 65
Portland Place, 52
Powis, Square, 63; Villas, 65
Preston Park; Bowling Green, 8; Rookery Rock Gardens, 10
Quadrophenia, 8, 22, 40
Queensbury Mews, 89
Queen's Park, 114, 123–126
Regency Fish Restaurant, 32
Regency Square, 32
Regency Townhouse, 103
Repton, Humphry, 79
Richmond Terrace, 67, 124
Rossini, Gioacchino,17
Royal Albion Hotel, 38
Royal Crescent, 40, 44, 46, 52
Royal Gardens, 118
Royal Pavilion, 7, 25, 38, 72–85
Russell, Dr Richard, 12, 14, 32, 123
Sackville-West, Vita, 57
Sassoon, Albert, 50
Sayers, Tom, 82
Scott, Edmund, 18
Scott, George Gilbert, 56
Sea Life Centre, 38
Selassie, Haile, 96
Sewers, 41
Ship Street, 36, 91, 96

Shoreham, 38
Sickert, Walter, 21, 35
Smith, George Albert, 110
Smith, Sydney, 72
Southover Street, 119
Spence, Sir Basil, 22
St Andrew's Church, 104–105
St Anne's Well, 102, 110, 123
St Bartholomew's Church, 18, 19
St Bartholomew's Priory, 88
St George's Chapel, 56
St Georges Road, 44
St James's Street, 44, 49
St John the Baptist, Church of, 57
St Michael's and All Angels Church, 70
St Nicholas Church, 15, 53, 68, 69
St Paul's Church, 96–97
St Peter's Church, 69, 124, 125, 126
St Stephen's Church, 20, 67
Stanford Estate, 107, 108
Steine, 26, 34, 49, 52, 79
Struve, Dr F. A., 123
Sussex Square, 44, 53, 54
Sydney Street, 85
Tamplin's Brewery, 119,122
Tettersell, Nicholas, 12, 20, 71
Thackeray, William 8, 19, 20
Theatre Royal, 72, 78, 79
Trafalgar Street, 82, 83
Turner, J.M.W., 17, 35, 36
Union Street, 91
University of Sussex, 22
Upper North Street, 60
Victoria Fountain, 46–47
Victoria, Queen, 53, 81
Victoria Road, 65
Ventnor Villas, 107
Volk, Magnus, 19, 36–38, 82
Wagner, Arthur, 17, 118, 119
Wagner, Rev. Henry, 17, 61, 69
Waterloo Street, 104
Waugh, Evelyn, 8
Wellington, Duke of, 71
Wellsbourne River, 11, 26
Wells, H.G., 38
Western Road, 58
Western Terrace, 67
Westphal, Sir George Augustus, 110
West Pier, 19, 26, 36, 99
Whitehawk Hill, 11
Wilde, Oscar, 21, 119
Wilds, Amon, 15, 46
Wilds, Amon Henry, 12, 16, 19, 46, 47, 58, 61, 62, 102, 107, 114, 118, 126
William IV, 53, 56, 81, 123, 124
Williamson, James, 110
Wyatt, James, 79
Wyndham, George, 36